# TELLING GOD'S STORY
# YEAR ONE: MEETING JESUS

## INSTRUCTOR TEXT AND TEACHING GUIDE

# TELLING GOD'S STORY
# YEAR ONE: MEETING JESUS

## INSTRUCTOR TEXT AND TEACHING GUIDE

PETER ENNS

**Olive Branch Books**
Charles City, Virginia

This book is to be used in conjunction with *Telling God's Story: Year One Activity Book: Student Guide and Activity Pages* (ISBN 978-1-933339-47-4), available at www.olivebranchbooks.net or wherever books are sold.

Publisher's Cataloging-In-Publication Data
(Prepared by The Donohue Group, Inc.)

Enns, Peter, 1961-   Telling God's story. Year One, Meeting Jesus : instructor text and teaching guide / Peter Enns.
   p. : ill. ; cm.

"This book is to be used in conjunction with Telling God's story: year one student guide and activity pages."
   Includes index.   ISBN: 978-1-933339-48-1    1. Jesus Christ--Biography--Study and teaching (Primary)  2. Jesus Christ--Teachings--Study and teaching (Primary) 3. Jesus Christ--Miracles--Study and teaching (Primary)  I. Title.

BT207 .E56 2010          2010927912
232

# Table of Contents

# Introduction

The Bible is primarily a God-centered story. It is not designed to be a "Book of Virtues" but a book that tells us who God is and what he has done. The Bible, in other words, is a story that begins with the dysfunction of the early chapters of Genesis, moves to God's dealings with a particular group of people—his chosen people, the Israelites—and then culminates in what God did through Jesus of Nazareth.

Who Jesus is and what he did are central to the Christian faith. That is why this curriculum begins with teaching children about Jesus. Of course, much of who Jesus is and what he did is rooted in the Old Testament, and we will certainly get to that—but in due time. It is good to remember that the first followers of Jesus were likely far less familiar with the Old Testament than we might think. There were no printed books back then. Peter and the others, when they were called by Jesus to follow him, did not have their Bibles open and may not even have been all that familiar with the Scripture's content.

When Jesus came on the scene he did not say, "OK, before I begin talking, please open up your Bibles and let me show you how all of this fits together." Rather, he came on the scene and just started being Jesus. And the point was made well enough.

So we will follow this pattern: beginning this curriculum by acquainting children with Jesus first and then letting the rest of the Bible fall into place. We are intentionally avoiding the "Bible story" approach, which starts with creation, Adam and Eve, the Flood, etc., as the basis of moral lessons. We are beginning at the culmination of the story, to see how all of this ends up—acquainting children with the most central truths of the Scripture before we go back to fill in the many interesting details.

A much fuller explanation of the methods behind this program is found in the core text for this series, *Telling God's Story: A Parents' Guide to Teaching the Bible.*

## Organization

The lessons for Year One are centered on understanding Jesus: who he was, what he did, and what he taught. The lessons organize the Gospel story into nine categories:

Stories Jesus Told
Miracles Jesus Did
Teachings of Jesus
The Sermon on the Mount
Jesus' Early Life
Jesus' Disciples
Opposition to Jesus
The End of Jesus' Life
The Rest of the Story

Aim to complete one lesson per week. This book is designed to be used along with *Telling God's Story, Year One Activity Book: Student Guide and Activity Pages*, which contains pictures, projects and other activities. You may wish to read the scripted lesson to the child on the first day as he or she colors the picture, and then to complete projects on the second and third days. Alternately, you may read the scripted lesson on the first day, complete the coloring picture on the second, and complete a chosen project on the third. In a group setting that meets once a week, plan to read the scripted lesson as the students color and then to conclude the day's study with one of the projects or games especially designed for group use.

Each of these categories will have four or five lessons, which means that you will spend four or five weeks on each category. (The last category has only three lessons.) The order is not unalterable, but neither is it random. We start with the stories Jesus told (parables) because this is one way that Jesus introduced himself to the people of his day. He also introduced himself to them through miracles and his various teachings, which are second and third on the list. These are the ways the people of Jesus' world got to know him, and it is a good way to introduce Jesus to your children, too.

The fourth category is the Sermon on the Mount, which is really a subset of the previous category ("Teachings of Jesus"). The Sermon on the Mount is so rich and well known, however, that it deserves a separate treatment. So the first four categories have one thing in common: they all pertain to what Jesus did and said to the people of his day. These were the ways people got to know him.

The next five categories are more biographical. Here the lessons will focus more on Jesus' life, beginning with his birth, then moving to his relationship with his disciples, the opposition he faced toward the end of his earthly ministry, and culminating in his death and resurrection. These categories are also important for children to get to know Jesus. Young students are often not taught the Gospel accounts of Jesus' life in a way that shows just how interesting and challenging the biblical message is. These last five categories will question some preconceptions, and therefore deepen our understanding of who Jesus is.

Even though the order of the lessons is intentional, parents should feel free to alter the order to suit their own purposes. For example, you might decide to work through "Jesus' Early Life" during the Christmas season and "The End of Jesus' Life" during Easter. The only strong suggestion I make is that each category be completed before moving onto another so that the lessons have a stronger sense of continuity ("next we are going to look at the miracles for Jesus for five weeks").

The purpose of this curriculum is to get to know Jesus better. In fact, it is very likely that as a parent or teacher, you may find yourself re-introduced to Jesus in a fresh way. This is why each lesson opens with a brief word of explanation to the parent; this will help you in helping your children process the content of the lessons.

Toward that end, you should spend a few moments reading the parent section ("What the Parent Should Know") the night before the lesson so you can ponder a bit, or if you prefer, read it right before the lesson so it is fresh in your mind—whatever works for you. The important thing is that you spend some time becoming familiar with the information so you can be of more help to your children. The purpose of these parent sections is to orient you to the biblical passage for that day. The parent sections are more detailed and complex than the scripted lessons; this will give you a broader handle on the issues surrounding the passage. It will also give you a greater vantage point from which to look at the lesson itself and, perhaps, to address questions that might come up.

All scriptural excerpts are drawn from the New International Version.

## Scope

Jesus is the primary subject of this curriculum for the first four years. We want to encourage parents and teachers not to feel as if the child's biblical education is being truncated by focusing on Jesus. Rather, *Telling God's Story* allows young students to get to know the central figure of the Christian faith in a way that conventional curricula do not do.

But this curriculum can't possibly cover all the parables of Jesus, or all the events of his life, or even all the events of Passion Week, in a single year. We assume that this curriculum is not your child's only exposure to the Bible. Your local church should provide your child's foundational education in the Gospel and Scripture. We are partnering with parents, teachers, and churches to teach the Gospel message; this gives us the freedom to approach the curriculum the way we do.

During each year of the elementary curriculum, the lessons repeat the nine categories, each year introducing new material and covering it in more depth. This means that a relatively short amount of time each year is spent on the pivotal events of Passion Week, Jesus' death, and the resurrection. We assume that your local church will play a major part in telling these stories and explaining their importance. However, it may seem a bit abrupt to end each year without looking in more detail at the crucifixion, the resurrection, and post-resurrection appearances of Jesus. So we also offer a supplemental unit to make sure those topics are adequately covered during each year of grades 1–4.

Unit 1

# Stories Jesus Told

For the Parent: Jesus was a master storyteller and preferred to use stories to introduce himself to his listeners. But this does not mean that the stories were easy to understand or that their meanings were self-evident. In fact, in one or two places, Jesus seems determined to obscure his message to those not prepared to hear it (Mark 4:11–12), probably because the secret of the kingdom is revealed only to those who responded to Jesus and followed him—to "insiders," so to speak. The parables are indeed a diverse group of passages that offer occasional interpretive challenges. But they are also concrete and show up everywhere in the Gospels. Jesus liked talking in parables, and this is why we begin with them as we introduce our children to his life.

**Lesson 1**

Luke 15:8–10

## God Is Joyful over You

*What the Parent Should Know: This parable is about the joy that God feels when a lost sinner is found. The child should understand that God is not indifferent or judgmental toward him—his response to God makes God himself joyful.*

*The joy in heaven over one sinner's repentance is compared by Jesus to a woman's joy at finding a lost silver coin. This coin is a Greek drachma, roughly equal to a day's wage. The losing of this coin was not merely an inconvenience. It was important to the woman's daily survival, and so she was understandably persistent in finding it. When we read that she lit a lamp to find the coin, we should not think of flicking on a light in the living room. Houses back then were dark and relatively windowless. A more appropriate modern analogy might be sweating in a crawl space with a flashlight in your mouth. And sweeping the house was not a matter of tidying up or running a vacuum cleaner, but rooting through the straw flooring that functioned as comfort and warmth. This woman was expending tremendous effort.*

*Jesus' parables are sometimes hard to understand. It is not always clear how the parts of the parable correspond to the lesson. This parable is a good example. For example, note that the coin represents a repentant sinner, which is a bit unexpected if you stop to think about it for a minute. Did the coin at first not want to be found, and then finally "repent" and present itself to the peasant woman? Of course not. Likewise, the woman who rejoiced seems to represent the angels in heaven who rejoice. But the woman rejoiced because she looked for and found the coin. There is no indication that the angels were ever looking for the repentant person.*

*It is important to realize that parables are not meant to have a one-to-one correspondence between each element of the story and each element of reality. Rather they are intended to create a vivid picture in our minds that is more than just the sum of its parts—a picture in which one particular truth stands out.*

*So the heart of this parable is the joy of the woman and the joy of angels in heaven. Just as for the woman the coin meant a lot, so, too, for the angels in heaven the repentant sinner means a lot. Our focus here is on that sense of joy.*

*Although God is not specifically mentioned in this parable, it is not at all a stretch, especially with a lesson geared toward first graders, to "inject" his presence, for his own joy is clearly presumed. Repentance is not something that God looks on begrudgingly. Rather, it gives him joy, a point that is emphasized in the very next parable of the Prodigal Son (see Luke 15:20–32 and how the father responds to the son's return).*

*Begin the lesson by reading aloud:*

Many of the people in Jesus' time were very poor. To help them understand more about God, Jesus told stories that they would really understand—like this one.

Suppose a woman has ten silver coins and loses one. Does she not light a lamp, sweep the house and search carefully until she finds it? And when she finds it, she calls her friends and neighbors together and says, "Rejoice with me; I have found my lost coin." In the same way, I tell you, there is rejoicing in the presence of the angels of God over one sinner who repents.

This poor woman lived in a small house that was very dark. She didn't even have windows. She had to light oil lamps when she wanted light. And there were no wooden floors or carpets either, just the ground covered with straw to keep things a bit warm and comfortable.

She had ten silver coins. That was a lot of money for her. One coin allowed her to buy food and oil for her lamp each day. So losing even just one silver coin meant that she would have no money for that day— no money for food or the oil she needed. That is why she looked for it desperately.

The house was dark, so she had to light an oil lamp so she could see, even though the oil cost money, too. She looked in every corner of her little house to find it. Imagine yourself in the darkest part of your house, maybe an attic or part of your basement. Imagine that all the lights went out and you had only a flashlight to find things. That is what it was like for this woman looking for her one little coin.

She even swept the floor so she could find the coin hidden in all that straw. Sometimes you drop something small on the floor, like a bead or a tiny Lego piece, or maybe a piece of a model you are gluing together. You get on your hands and knees, but it is so hard to find. It blends right in with the carpet, or maybe it rolled under a sofa. Imagine if your whole house had straw on the floor instead of carpets or wood or linoleum. It would take you forever to find anything.

It was very slow work, but the woman kept looking until she found the coin. And when she did, she was so happy she went and told her friends and neighbors.

This woman felt the way you would feel if you lost something important to you. Imagine getting ready to go on a long vacation with your family. Right before you leave, and everyone is getting into the car, you realize that you can't find your favorite toy or book or stuffed animal— the one you take with you everywhere. There is NO WAY you are getting into that car until you find it! So you and your family go back inside and go through the whole house looking until you find it. And when you do, you feel filled with joy and relief.

Lesson 1: God Is Joyful over You

God wants us to love him and to know him. And when we do, God feels the same kind of joy this woman had when she found that precious coin. The coin was something she *longed* to have. And God longs for us in the same way. God is full of joy about us.

## Lesson 2

## Luke 18:1–8

## Don't Give Up When You Pray

*What the Parent Should Know: This parable is about God wanting us to keep bringing our concerns to him. No explanation of the different elements in this parable is given—other than that God will not lose patience or become annoyed, like the judge in this parable.*

*In Jesus' times, judges were figures of authority whose responsibility it was to make sure that justice was carried out. Injustice, in the form of taking advantage of the poor and others (like the widow in this story) who had no social clout, was rampant. The judge in this story had no compulsion to be just, since he "neither feared God nor cared about men." This put people like the widow of the story in a position of oppression from which there was no means of escape, no higher court of appeal. She had no choice but to be persistent in making her appeal in the hope that the judge would change his mind.*

*Jesus' point here is that even such an unjust judge will eventually be worn down by a widow's persistence. And if this can be expected with an unjust judge, how much more reliable is God, the supremely just judge? The answer may not come immediately; even with God, persistence is a virtue. But unlike with the unjust judge, the one who appeals to God can rest assured that the prayer is indeed being heard from the very beginning.*

*Persistence, therefore, is not a futile banging of one's head against the wall. It is, for whatever reason, a dimension of prayer. Prayer is an exercise in persistence. So to paraphrase Jesus' point, when in praying there is no answer immediately forthcoming, do not picture in your mind an unjust God who has turned a deaf ear. Picture instead a listening and responsive God.*

*Now, what Jesus does not answer is why such persistence in prayer has to happen in the first place. Why, after all, does God not show how completely different he is from the unjust judge by answering swiftly? Jesus does not address that here, but we can presume that persistence is valued by him because it does something for us. It is part of our training, a way in which we learn to live lives of dependence on God. And so the need for persistence is something we should expect.*

*Jesus is telling the people not to misinterpret the need for persistence as "God doesn't care"—a reaction that was natural then, and is still natural now. Rather, it is precisely because God is just and caring that persistence will pay off. And so one should "always pray and not give up" (v. 1).*

*Begin the lesson by reading aloud:*

Jesus tells this story about a widow who needed help.

> Then Jesus told his disciples a parable to show them that they should always pray and not give up. He said: "In a certain town there was a judge who neither feared God nor cared about men. And there was a widow in that town who kept coming to him with the plea, 'Grant me justice against my adversary.'
>
> "For some time he refused. But finally he said to himself, 'Even though I don't fear God or care about men, yet because this widow keeps bothering me, I will see that she gets justice, so that she won't eventually wear me out with her coming!'"
>
> And the Lord said, "Listen to what the unjust judge says. And will not God bring about justice for his chosen ones, who cry out to him day and night? Will he keep putting them off? I tell you, he will see that they get justice, and quickly. However, when the Son of Man comes, will he find faith on the earth?"

In Jesus' day, it was especially difficult to be a widow. (A widow is a woman whose husband has died.) It is always sad to be a widow, but back then a widow was all alone. Widows often had to rely on the kindness of strangers just to get by day to day. This is because women did not have the same rights that men had. They couldn't work to support themselves, and so they had to depend on first their fathers and then their husbands. They couldn't care for themselves.

If someone wanted to be unfair to a widow or mistreat her, she had no family to go to for help. She had to rely on the goodness and fairness of people called judges. Their job was to make sure people were treated fairly. Poor and desperate people who were being treated badly could go to the judges when they needed help.

In this story, a widow is having some trouble with someone (Jesus doesn't tell us what's wrong because that is not important for the story).

She goes to the judge in town, but he is not good or fair. The widow is counting on the judge to help her. But the judge refuses to do his duty. He refuses to listen to her.

Has anyone ever done something to you that was unfair and wrong? Imagine that you're at a party or a picnic or some family gathering. An older child starts to pick on you, push you around, and finally takes away something that is yours.

When that happens you usually find a grown-up and ask for help. Now imagine that you go up to an adult—an uncle or aunt, or maybe even your parent—and tell them what happened. But the grown-up just shrugs and walks away. Your friends can't help you. No one else can help you. You would feel angry and frustrated because someone did something very wrong to you, and the one person who is supposed to help doesn't.

That is what this widow felt like. But what does she do? She has no choice: she has to keep going back, again and again, to ask for help, and she doesn't stop until the judge is so tired of her asking the same old thing, that he helps her.

Jesus tells us this story to show us what God is like—and what God is *not* like. God is a judge, too—someone you go to when you need help. But God is not anything like the judge in this story. He really listens to us and cares for us. He does not ignore us!

But Jesus also tells us this story to show us something about *us*. When we ask God for something, we are not supposed to give up. The way the widow in the story behaves is the way *we* are supposed to be. God wants us to keep asking and keep asking and keep asking.

This story doesn't answer all our questions. For one thing, it doesn't tell us *why* our prayers aren't immediately answered. We don't always know why. But the message of this story is very clear. Jesus tells us that we must be persistent when we pray. If we don't see an answer to our prayer, it doesn't mean that God is like a bad judge. Instead, it means that God wants us to keep asking.

# Matthew 13:31–33

# Small Beginnings, Big Results

*What the Parent Should Know: The general point of these two related parables is that the kingdom of heaven may have an unimpressive beginning but will have a big effect. Each element mentioned (mustard seed and yeast) adds its own dimension to the lesson. Jesus used such everyday things to explain the unfamiliar and mysterious.*

*First, what exactly is the "kingdom of heaven"? This is commonly misunderstood as a statement about the next life, but this is not at all on Jesus' mind here. He instead means the kingdom that God is working to build in the here and now. Perhaps it would be better to think of it as a kingdom* from *heaven, or perhaps a kingdom peopled by citizens whose behavior is marked by a heavenly character. In this sense, Jesus is consistent with much of Old Testament hope, that God would reign on earth through his anointed king (messiah) and restore order and godliness to his people. Jesus came to make that happen. Ultimately the kingdom of God will be fulfilled in the new people of God, the church, made up of Jew and Gentile together, not just the Israelites. These are the members of the kingdom Jesus has in mind.*

*The mustard was consided the smallest seed in Jesus' day (it measures 2 mm, or about .08 inches), but it grew into a tree several feet high. Likewise, the kingdom of heaven begins with one person: Jesus, like a seed, is placed in the ground (in death), but the result is an immense people of God. People from all nations will come and "perch" in the "branches" of the kingdom. In both cases, the end result is wholly unexpected, given the small beginnings.*

*A very small amount of yeast makes dough rise. In the New Testament, yeast is often an indication of some negative influence, but not here. Just as the mustard seed is small, the yeast is inconspicuous; it is mixed in thoroughly with the flour and is unnoticed. Nevertheless, the yeast has a pervasive influence on the lump of dough: it is the ingredient that allows the dough to rise. Without it, there is no bread. So, too, the Gospel will have a permeating influence wherever it is found.*

*The kingdom of heaven will be built in unexpected ways and exceed all expectations that the people in Jesus' time may have had. This is also true for us today. What God is doing in our lives and through us often seems tiny and unimportant, but over time the results are much bigger and more amazing than we can possibly expect.*

*Begin by reading aloud:*

> He told them another parable: "The kingdom of heaven is like a mustard seed, which a man took and planted in his field. Though it is the smallest of all your seeds, yet when it grows, it is the largest of garden plants and becomes a tree, so that the birds of the air come and perch in its branches."
>
> He told them still another parable: "The kingdom of heaven is like yeast that a woman took and mixed into a large amount of flour until it worked all through the dough."

One tiny red lollipop. That's all it takes. That one lollipop slips out of your pocket on laundry day and winds up mixed in with all the white towels, sheets, and underwear. And what happens? When you take the laundry out, that red lollipop has mixed in with all of the laundry, and you have pink towels, sheets, and underwear.

This is not fun, unless you really like the color pink.

Small actions and tiny objects can make a big difference. This is what Jesus is talking about here. A mustard seed is very, very small, about two millimeters (see how small it is on a ruler). But it can grow into a tree that would probably go through the ceiling in your house. Something so big from something so small!

And when you are baking bread, if you want the dough to rise, you take a big lump of dough and add a little bit of yeast to it. (Yeast is a fungus that mixes together with the dough and makes the dough expand.) All you need is a tiny pinch of yeast; it spreads throughout the whole lump of dough.

Jesus came to teach people about God. He was only one man in a world full of people, too many people to count. In this story, Jesus is saying that his kingdom begins with just him. Just one person. But it will grow into something very big.

Jesus calls this big result the "kingdom of heaven." When he says this, Jesus isn't talking about going to heaven after you die, or a kingdom that is up in the sky somewhere. "Kingdom of heaven" means a kingdom here on earth that looks the way God, who is in heaven, wants it to look.

This kingdom has already begun to grow on earth. Today, there are people all over the world who believe in Jesus and follow what he taught. And everything started with that one man.

## Lesson 4

# God Loves a Humble Heart

*What the Parent Should Know: This well-known parable demonstrates, as do many others (for example, the sheep and the goats in Matthew 25:31–46), the type of "religion" Jesus was interested in. Much of Jesus' teaching centered on compassion, love, forgiveness, self-denial, and (as here) humility. The counterintuitive nature of this parable is not always appreciated: God is actually more pleased with a sinner who knows about and is sorry for his sinful nature, than someone who is acting properly and morally but who thinks that his good deeds are something to brag about.*

*The Pharisee is doing pretty well by the standards of the day. He is indeed thankful that he is not a robber, evildoer (someone who does harm to others), adulterer, or tax collector. The first three are dealt with in Jewish law. Adulterers were put to death, robbers had to make restitution for what they took (and then some), and doing evil to others was met with penalties that matched the crime (hence, "eye for an eye" as we read in Exodus 21:24).*

*In Jesus' day, tax collectors were Jews who collected taxes for their hated oppressors, the Romans. Tax collectors were considered dishonest traitors to their own people and, along with lepers, were about as loathed a group of people as you could find.*

*We have our modern-day tax collectors. How many of us have not said, "Lord, I may not be perfect, but I am glad I am not a mass murderer, drug dealer, child molester," etc.?*

*But this Pharisee is none of those things. In fact, he goes above and beyond the call of duty. He fasts twice a week, whereas the Law only requires fasting once a year, on the Day of Atonement. And he tithes ten percent of all he has, not just what he earns. By all counts, he is genuinely a good man. He is, to use the biblical term, righteous. In the Bible, "righteousness" is not an abstract quality (like a "clean soul"), as it is sometimes understood by Christians today. "Righteousness" was doing the right thing, being "in the right" in one's actions. In today's language we might say something like "he is a good man" to describe someone who keeps the law, does right by other people, doesn't cheat, etc. This is someone you can trust and rely on.*

*This Pharisee is confident in his own righteousness. But it is important to remember: this is a real righteousness the Pharisee has, not a fake one. He is a good man, doing what Israel's law required of him. So what is the problem?*

*The Pharisee is righteous, but righteousness is not what puts you in good standing with God.*

*This is also true in the Old Testament. The Law was the standard of Israel's righteousness. But adhering to the Law is not what put Israelites in good standing with Yahweh. Remember the exodus from Egypt: God saved the Israelites first and then gave them the law on Mount Sinai. The purpose of the Law was not to give the Israelites a standard of conduct so they could be God's people somehow. They already were God's people: he had delivered them from Egypt. To put it in more contemporary language, the Law is not a way to "get saved," neither in the New Testament nor in the Old. Rather, the Law is what is given to saved people. We see this in the Ten Commandments. Before any command is given, the people are reminded of who God is and what he did: "I am the LORD your God who brought you out of Egypt, out of the land of slavery." The commandments that follow are based on God's previous saving act.*

*By contrast, the tax collector seems to understand this. He has actually sinned by fleecing his people, and so he goes back to his saving God, in humility, and asks for God's mercy. The issue here is not that the Pharisee is really a sinner deep down, just like the tax collector, and so none of the good things he does matter—they do matter. The Pharisee really is righteous—he does right things—and the tax collector really was a sinner.*

*What separates them is where they place their confidence in their relationship with God. None of what the Pharisee does will reflect a godly life if it is not based on humility toward the very God who saved him to enable him to do those things. Likewise, the tax collector's sin is not irrelevant to God ("Hey, since you're humble, go right on ahead and be a tax collector"). Rather, the point of the parable is that a humble sinner has a clearer understanding of the heart of God and is closer to the "kingdom of heaven" than a (truly) righteous person who puts his confidence in himself.*

*Begin by reading aloud:*

> To some who were confident of their own righteousness and looked down on everybody else, Jesus told this parable: "Two men went up to the temple to pray, one a Pharisee and the other a tax collector. The Pharisee stood up and prayed about himself: 'God, I thank you that I am not like other men—robbers, evildoers, adulterers—or even like this tax collector. I fast twice a week and give a tenth of all I get.'

Lesson 4: God Loves a Humble Heart

"But the tax collector stood at a distance. He would not even look up to heaven, but beat his breast and said, 'God, have mercy on me, a sinner.'

"I tell you that this man, rather than the other, went home justified before God. For everyone who exalts himself will be humbled, and he who humbles himself will be exalted."

You probably know lots of people who think they are good at something, like a sport, or dancing, or art. And you know what—they *are* good, too. Maybe they practice a lot or were born with a lot of talent.

Tonya and Amanda are both soccer players. Tonya is not very good at soccer. It doesn't come easily to her. She has to work hard. She comes to practice every day and practices at home, too. She wants to be better, but it is hard. Amanda is very good at any sport she tries. It seems that she doesn't even have to try or practice. She just runs out onto the field and she is the best on the team.

Amanda is a great soccer player, but she brags about herself a lot. Just last week Amanda scored the winning goal in a very big game. Everyone was happy and cheering. But Amanda wasn't humble at all. She was cocky and even bragged about it in school for the next few days, telling the other kids how great she is and how her team couldn't have won without her.

It's great to be good at something, but bragging about it all the time can become annoying. The other girls don't like Amanda very much because she is so full of herself. They just want to keep away from her.

Amanda is like the Pharisee in Jesus' story. He is telling God how good a person he is. The Pharisee is a very good man—just like Amanda is truly a good soccer player. The Pharisee doesn't rob or hurt anyone. In fact, he fasts a lot and tithes more than he has to (both are things the Old Testament requires Jews to do). He spends his time the way he should, doing the kinds of things that God wants his people to do. But the Pharisee looks down on everybody else. He thinks he is a better friend of God, simply because of the good things he does.

The tax collector in the parable is very different. Tax collectors were Jews who collected taxes from their own people for the Roman government. No one wanted to be around them. This tax collector is not a very good person at all, but he knows it. He is humble.

Maybe the Pharisee this he has to make sure he is good enough for God. But Jesus tells us that being humble is more important to God than just being good. Why is being humble important to God? Because God

**Lesson 4: God Loves a Humble Heart**

21

wants us to understand how much he loves us. Yes, he wants us to follow his commands—but he loves us *just because he loves us.*

<table>
<tr><td>**Lesson**<br>**5**</td><td>**Matthew 18:12–14**<br><br>**Lost Sheep**</td></tr>
</table>

*What the Parent Should Know: The parable of the lost sheep concerns those who are already in the family of God but have wandered away. It is not an evangelistic parable, where the lost sheep represents the unsaved. It is an illustration of God's love and care for his own people.*

*The larger context of this brief but well-known passage concerns children and the requirement to become "like a child" in order to be a member of Jesus' kingdom (18:1–9). Jesus refers to "little children" or "little ones" in 18:3, 5, and 6. He continues this thought in v. 10 and then at the end of our passage, in v. 14.*

*In this parable, Jesus has foremost in his mind "little ones" who have been led astray and the joy of the shepherd when such a one who is led astray returns to the fold. "Little ones" in this parable does not only mean literal young children; it also means those who have heeded Jesus' claim in v. 4 and have become "like little children" (v. 3) in order to follow Jesus.*

*The shepherd/sheep metaphor is a common one in the Bible for God and his people (e.g., Psalm 23). It is also sometimes used (by extension) for some representative of God such as Moses (Psalm 77:20). Finding the lost sheep, therefore, is not about a metaphor for unbelievers coming to faith. The lost sheep represents a follower who is either straying for some reason and in need of correction, or perhaps the subject of mistreatment or oppression (as were the sheep Israel in Egypt).*

*The lost sheep should be in the fold but has "wandered away" (v. 12) for some unstated reason. The shepherd is happier at retrieving that lost sheep than simply delighting in the others who remain. He is not willing that any of his sheep should be lost. This is an important dimension of the Gospel that can sometimes get lost in the shuffle. Too often we focus only on God's love in Christ that saves us, without remembering the love of God that keeps us saved. In Romans 5:9–11, Paul puts it this way: if we were once reconciled to*

*God when we were enemies of God, don't you think that God will do what is needed to make sure, now that we are reconciled to God, that we stay that way?*

*Thus, this parable is about the steadiness of God's love.*

*Begin by reading aloud:*

> "What do you think? If a man owns a hundred sheep, and one of them wanders away, will he not leave the ninety-nine on the hills and go to look for the one that wandered off? And if he finds it, I tell you the truth, he is happier about that one sheep than about the ninety-nine that did not wander off. In the same way your Father in heaven is not willing that any of these little ones should be lost."

The big day is here. You are taking a trip to an amusement park. You are leaving early in the morning and getting back late at night. The amusement park is huge. It has two enormous Ferris wheels, and rides that whip you around, twist you about, and swing you back and forth.

You are going with a lot of other children from church. A few parents are going to help, and the youth pastor is in charge of everything.

When you get there, you can't believe your eyes. It is SO big, bigger than you thought possible. And there is so much to do, you hardly know where to start. But before you run off to have the time of your life, the pastor calls you all together. "We have to stick together. This is a very big amusement park, and we don't want anyone getting lost. DON'T just go off on your own!"

But there is always someone who doesn't listen. After a while, when you've had the chance to go on some rides and have an ice cream, someone asks, "Where's Eddie?" No one knows. "Maybe he's in the bathroom, or in the arcade?" A parent checks, but no Eddie.

You wait a while to see if he'll just come wandering back (Eddie likes to wander). Still, no Eddie.

Now people are starting to worry. "What if he's really lost and he doesn't know where we are?" The day started out so great, but now all anyone can think about is this one child, Eddie, who is lost somewhere in the park.

So the pastor says, "OK. Here's what we're going to do. No more rides or ice cream for anyone until we find Eddie. Nothing is more important than finding him right now. He can't be far. Let's break up into groups and look for him."

You all look for Eddie for a long time. It seems like forever. Then, finally, someone finds him. He is sitting on a bench, under a shady tree, petting someone's dog. You hear the joyful shouts: "There you are, Eddie!"

Everyone is so relieved to see Eddie again. No one was thinking about the rides or the ice cream. You were all thinking of only one thing: finding Eddie.

This is like the story Jesus tells. He talks about a shepherd who has a hundred sheep and one gets lost. It is the shepherd's job to keep all the sheep with him, safe and sound, but this one sheep goes his own way. So the shepherd stops everything he's doing and looks and looks until he finds the lost sheep.

Jesus is saying that all those who believe in him are like sheep, and Jesus is the shepherd. Sometimes "sheep" like us wander away. We forget what Jesus has taught us in the Bible. Maybe we stop thinking about Jesus and his love for us.

But Jesus is saying here that he goes on loving each and every one of his sheep, even when they wander off. He is not upset or angry. Instead, he is like the good shepherd in the story—he only wants to find us again.

# Unit 2

# Miracles Jesus Did

For the Parent: Jesus' miracles were another means of introducing himself to the people of his time. They were not, however, merely displays of strength or power, intended to draw attention to himself. And the miracles did not "prove" that Jesus was divine. (Similar abilities were displayed by Moses and Elijah, for example.)

Rather, by performing miracles, Jesus was drawing attention to his role as God's special servant. He was demonstrating that his "connection" with God was indeed unique and that he was, therefore, sent by God to do his work. The miracles established in the eyes of the people (and the disciples, see John 2:11 in Lesson 6) that Jesus had God's authority behind him, which is why John refers to them as "signs" (v. 11). As we see so often in the Gospels, Jesus' authority was the very thing that the religious leaders kept challenging.

Jesus' miracles can be understood from two angles. First, miracles show Jesus' control over the powers of creation. When Jesus controls wind and water, heals the sick, and raises the dead, he is showing his ability to manipulate the forces of creation, just as Yahweh, the Father God and Creator, does in the Old Testament. These miracles display the intimacy between the Father and Son, and so express what is said succinctly in Colossians 1:16: "all things were created by him and for him."

Second, healings are part of the Old Testament picture of the coming messiah. A "messiah" in the Old Testament was someone who was "anointed" (this is what the Hebrew word means), or chosen, to be a representative of God in some respect. Typically, the messianic role was one fulfilled by kings: they were all anointed with oil to rule the people for God. So performing miracles was a part of Jesus' messianic role—he was representing God to the people. We see this, for example, in Jesus' response to John the Baptist's question in Luke 7:22 and in Old Testament passages such as Isaiah 35:3–6. The miracles are loud exclamations that the kingdom of God, hinted at in various portions of the Old Testament, had indeed arrived in the person of Jesus.

**Lesson**

**6**

# John 2:1–11

# Jesus' First Miracle

*What the Parent Should Know: Jesus' first public miracle in the Gospel of John seems a bit, well, unexceptional. One might have expected a healing or maybe even raising someone from the dead. Instead, we find Jesus as a guest at a wedding where the hosts didn't plan ahead well enough and ran out of wine.*

*The normal solution for this would be for the host to run out and buy some. But instead we read that Mary brought the issue to Jesus' attention. Jesus didn't seem anxious to solve the problem; his main objection was that his "time had not yet come" (v. 4). It is clear that Mary knew very well that Jesus could handle this problem easily, but Jesus was concerned about drawing attention to himself in such a way, and at such an early moment in his ministry. This is actually a concern of his throughout the Gospels, that he not play his hand too soon. If he did, people would pay too much attention to the miracles themselves, rather than allowing the miracles to draw attention to Jesus as God's servant.*

*In a delightful mother-son exchange, Jesus seems to tell Mary to leave him alone, but Mary reads between the lines, as mothers are so good at doing, and tells the servants to do as he says. And so Jesus turns water into wine, but it is a compromise of sorts. Only his disciples and the servants know what he did. He does not stand up on the table, clink the glass with his fork, and make an announcement. He does it quietly and uses the moment as an opportunity to establish his identity to his disciples. They see at that point that Jesus is much more than a run-of-the-mill rabbi, and that he is worthy of their trust and allegiance—or as John puts it, "He thus revealed his glory and the disciples put their faith in him" (v. 11). Jesus has authority over the elements of creation and can change one thing into another.*

*You may want to explain to the student that the "disciples" were men who followed Jesus and learned from him.*

*Begin by reading aloud:*

> On the third day a wedding took place at Cana in Galilee. Jesus' mother was there, and Jesus and his disciples had also been invited to the wedding. When the wine was gone, Jesus' mother said to him, "They have no more wine."
>
> "Dear woman, why do you involve me?" Jesus replied, "My time has not yet come."
>
> His mother said to the servants, "Do whatever he tells you."
>
> Nearby stood six stone water jars, the kind used by the Jews for ceremonial washing, each holding from twenty to thirty gallons. Jesus said to the servants, "Fill the jars with water"; so they filled them to the brim.
>
> Then he told them, "Now draw some out and take it to the master of the banquet."
>
> They did so, and the master of the banquet tasted the water that had been turned into wine. He did not realize where it had come from, though the servants who had drawn the water knew. Then he called the bridegroom aside and said, "Everyone brings out the choice wine first and then the cheaper wine after the guests have had too much to drink; but you have saved the best till now."
>
> This, the first of his miraculous signs, Jesus performed in Cana of Galilee. He thus revealed his glory, and his disciples put their faith in him.

Did your mother ever give you something to drink that you really didn't like? Maybe she made you drink water when you really wanted soda or juice. Wouldn't it be great if you could just snap your fingers and turn that water into whatever you wanted? That would be amazing (and fun).

You can't actually turn the water into something else. But that's what Jesus did in his first miracle. He turned water into wine at a wedding in the town of Cana.

When Jesus' mother asked him to help, he didn't agree immediately. It's not that he didn't want to help. But he knew that if people saw what he could do, they might think he was like a magician who does tricks. He knew that if people saw his power, they would want to be around him just so that they could get things from him.

Jesus knew that if people started wanting to be around him *just* because he could do miracles, they might not listen to what he had to teach them about God. So he didn't tell anyone what he was doing. Only the disciples and a few servants saw that Jesus turned the water into wine. Jesus kept the miracle secret from everyone else at the wedding.

When the disciples saw the miracle, they began to understand that Jesus really had power from God to do things no one else could do. He could change water to wine. Later, after he had spent some time teaching the people, Jesus would do other miracles. He would heal people who were sick and feed thousands of people with just a little food.

These miracles showed that Jesus had power over everything created on earth—just like God. God is the Creator. He made everything and has power over it. And the miracles of Jesus, beginning with the water turned into wine, showed that Jesus too had power over all of creation.

## Lesson 7

### Matthew 8:23–27

### Jesus Controls the Weather

*What the Parent Should Know: This is one of the better-known miracles of Jesus, and for good reason: Jesus begins to control the weather, to the amazement of his disciples. Up to now, his ministry has been characterized by some healings (which are enough to make one take notice) and some powerful and challenging speeches. But this act of calming the storm is different, for it shows Jesus' ability to control the elements of the created order.*

*When wind and water are put back in their place, so to speak, we should be reminded of the parting of the Red Sea by Moses. Here, too, God's people are saved from a watery threat. The miracle also calls to mind the story of Noah, where another watery threat comes to naught. And ultimately, the controlling of the elements of creation takes us back to Genesis 1, where God brought order by controlling the swirling, chaotic, primeval waters (called "the deep" in some English translations of Genesis 1:2).*

*Jesus' miracle here makes very clear that Jesus' ministry is a redemptive event, following the pattern of these other big redemptive events in the Old*

Testament. The miracle also sets Jesus apart as one who truly has the right to be heard: he does things that only God can be said to do, hence the disciples' reaction "What kind of man is this?" Even though the disciples already know that they had to turn to Jesus for help ("Lord, save us!"), they are now beginning to understand that he is more than they might have thought—a napping, drowsy messiah at one moment, who can roll out of bed, so to speak, and control nature by the words of his mouth.

As we saw in Lesson 6, this display of Jesus' power over creation is only revealed to his disciples. One can imagine the "media circus" that would have ensued had such displays been the center of Jesus' public ministry. What Jesus was about was not the miracles themselves. Rather, the miracles served a larger purpose—they confirmed the divine authority of his words and deeds.

Begin by reading aloud:

Before I read you the passage we're going to learn about today, let me tell you what comes just before it. Jesus had been talking to crowds of people. There was a lot of confusion around Jesus—the crowd had begun to push and shove to see him—and Jesus wanted to teach something to only the disciples. So he told the disciples that they should all take fishing boats (many of the disciples had been fishermen before they began to follow Jesus, so they knew all about boats) and cross over to the other side of the lake (the Sea of Galilee).

> Then he got into the boat and his disciples followed him. Without warning, a furious storm came up on the lake, so that the waves swept over the boat. But Jesus was sleeping. The disciples went and woke him, saying, "Lord, save us! We're going to drown!"
>
> He replied, "You of little faith, why are you so afraid?" Then he got up and rebuked the winds and the waves, and it was completely calm.
>
> The men were amazed and asked, "What kind of man is this? Even the winds and the waves obey him!"

It is really disappointing to have a nice day planned only to have it ruined by the weather. Maybe you have a picnic planned, or you are going to the fair, or you have a soccer or baseball game to play. And then it rains, and everything is ruined.

You might wish that you could just make the rain stop, but of course you can't. When it rains it rains, and there isn't anything you can do about it. You might just as well jump over the moon as make the rain stop. You simply have to wait.

That's why this is such an amazing story. Jesus and his disciples are on a boat crossing the Sea of Galilee. All of a sudden a big storm comes and tosses the boat back and forth. The storm is so bad that the disciples are afraid they will drown. If you have ever been outside in a really bad storm—not even in a boat, but just out in the open, in a big field or at the shore—you know how frightening it can be.

But the storm didn't frighten Jesus at all. In fact, he was taking a nap!

When Jesus controls the storm, he is showing the disciples that he has God's power. God is the only one who has the power to make creation do what he wants. Jesus can control the weather because he is God's son.

This story doesn't mean that every time something bad happens, Jesus will make it better right away. Instead, it shows us that Jesus has God's power.

### Lesson 8

## Luke 9:10–17

## Five Loaves and Two Fish

*What the Parent Should Know: Jesus and the disciples had intended to take a bit of a break in the town of Bethsaida (on the Sea of Galilee), but a crowd followed them nonetheless. So Jesus spent the better part of a day talking to them about the kingdom he was building, the kingdom of God (v. 11). The news that Jesus came to build this kingdom is called the Gospel or "good news" (see Luke 9:6).*

*The crowd numbered about 5,000 men, many more if you included women and children. They refused to leave, and the disciples were apparently concerned that they would not have enough for them to eat. They told Jesus to send them away, but he had something different in mind: "You give them something to eat." But with only five loaves and two fish, the disciples' only option as far as they could see, was to go to town and do some shopping. That option was ridiculous from a financial point of view, and one wonders if there is even a hint of sarcasm in the disciples' voices.*

*Of course, Jesus had other ideas. Once again, the feeding of the 5,000 is more than just a show of power on Jesus' part: Jesus's miracle is patterned after the Old Testament. This miracle calls to mind the provision of manna and quail of the Exodus generation (note that that happened in the desert [Exodus 16:1], and the feeding of the 5,000 occurred in a "remote place" [Luke 9:12].) The miracle is also clearly reminiscent of Elisha's feeding of the 100 (2 Kings 4:42–44).*

*Jesus sees his ministry as a continuation of what God had been doing in the Old Testament. The salvation seen in glimpses in the Old Testament is clearly expressed in Jesus, the messiah. Furthermore, the heart of the miracle is not the fact that Jesus gave thanks, and poof, all this food appeared ("so be sure to give thanks for your food," etc.). We must note, rather, that the disciples themselves were involved in this miracle. They had just been commissioned by God (Luke 9:1–9), and through the miracle of the loaves and fish, Jesus was letting them know that they would have a major role in spreading the good news of the coming of the kingdom of God.*

*The valuable lesson to be learned from this parable is that the Lord works through his people to show the Gospel to the world. We are his instruments, his servants, in mediating the good news to others. We may often pray "Lord, please do X." Sometimes his response is, "You do it, although I am with you."*

*Begin by reading aloud:*

In the story just before this one, Jesus had sent his disciples out to the villages. He gave them the power to do all sorts of miracles and to speak about Jesus with courage. The Bible does not say how long they were away, but it was long enough for Herod, the ruler of Galilee, to hear about it.

When the disciples returned, Jesus took them out to the desert, probably to talk privately about all that they saw and did in the villages. But the people found out where they were going and followed them. That is why there were so many people to feed.

Now I'll read you the story from Luke 9:

> When the apostles returned, they reported to Jesus what they had done. Then he took them with him and they withdrew by themselves to a town called Bethsaida, but the crowds learned about it and followed him. He welcomed them and spoke to them about the kingdom of God, and healed those who needed healing.
>
> Late in the afternoon the Twelve came to him and said, "Send the crowd away so they can go to the surrounding villages and countryside and find food and lodging, because we are in a remote place here."
>
> He replied, "You give them something to eat."

**Lesson 8: Five Loaves and Two Fish**

They answered, "We have only five loaves of bread and two fish—unless we go and buy food for all this crowd." (About five thousand men were there.)

But he said to his disciples, "Have them sit down in groups of about fifty each." The disciples did so, and everybody sat down. Taking the five loaves and the two fish and looking up to heaven, he gave thanks and broke them. Then he gave them to the disciples to set before the people. They all ate and were satisfied, and the disciples picked up twelve basketfuls of broken pieces that were left over.

We learn all sorts of new things from our parents and grandparents. Sometimes parents teach their children to do things like cook and bake, or fix things that are broken, or build a tree house. Sometimes grandparents help their grandchildren learn how to use a piece of equipment like a drill or a sewing machine.

When you first learn something new, the person who is teaching you is right there showing you how to do it. If you are learning how to bake a cake, maybe your mother or father helps you measure the ingredients. They may stand next to you and make sure that the oven is turned on and at the right temperature. They may help you find the right pans and utensils to use. Maybe they help you find what you need in the refrigerator or in the cupboards.

But after you do something new a few times, you might want to try it on your own, without quite so much help. Maybe you want to measure the ingredients yourself, and mix them without your mother or father watching your every step, telling you what to do.

If you forget how to do something, or you are not sure what to do, you might ask your mother or father for help. But as you grow older, they might not help you every time. It might be time for you to remember what you were taught and to try your best to do it. You might say, "Mom, help me measure the flour." But she might answer, "No, I want you to do this on your own this time."

This is what is happening with Jesus and his disciples. There are too many people to feed, and the disciples tell Jesus, "You'd better find some way to feed them, Jesus. You should send them away to the town so they can buy something to eat." The disciples wanted Jesus to do something, but Jesus said, "No, YOU do something."

Why would Jesus say that? Because these were his disciples and he had been teaching them about God for quite a while now. It was time for the disciples to do something, too. That is why Jesus told the disciples to

Lesson 8: Five Loaves and Two Fish

make the people sit down and to give them the bread and the fish, and then to gather all the food that was left over.

Jesus did the miracle of providing the food—but the disciples were the ones who gave out the food. Jesus was teaching them that it was not just *his* job to show people that he was the Son of God. That was their job, too!

## Lesson 9

## Mark 6:45–52

## Jesus Walks on the Water

*What the Parent Should Know: Just as Jesus calmed the storm (Lesson 7), Jesus here controls the elements as he walks on the water. This is not a random show of power, as if Jesus is thinking, "What can I do to convince people of who I am?" It is highly symbolic.*

*Note that in the previous passage in Mark, Jesus had just fed the 5,000 (the same story we just read in Lesson 8, as told by Luke). He told the disciples to go on ahead while he dismissed the crowd and then went into the hills to pray. Probably, the crowd intended to make him their king, i.e., their messiah. This confusion over what kind of king Jesus would be is a common theme in the Gospels.*

*But Jesus has other intentions. He goes to pray and then goes out to meet his disciples by walking to them out in the middle of the lake. Like Yahweh in the Old Testament, Jesus is showing his mastery over the seas (e.g., Psalm 89:9). He is signaling, in other words, the kind of king he is. Not a political king, but a king with the power of God over creation.*

*Another recurring theme in the Gospels that we see here is the disciples' slowness to recognize who was among them. Had they truly understood the miracle of the loaves, they would not have been afraid when they saw Jesus walking to them. But they hadn't understood that Jesus controls the elements of nature—whether bread, storms, water, sickness, etc. Again, the miracles are not just Jesus flexing his muscles, but his calling card to show what kind of messiah/king he is. All of these miracles show that God is with him and that the long-awaited messianic age has dawned.*

*It is important for children to keep learning what the Gospels are so intent to portray, that Jesus claims a unique relationship with God, and that his miracles have the purpose of establishing his identity.*

*Begin by reading aloud:*

Before I read you the passage we're going to learn about today, let me remind you what comes just before it. Jesus had just finished feeding more than 5,000 people with only two fish and five loaves of bread. Right after that, Jesus told his disciples to get into a boat and go to the town of Bethsaida. This was a town near the Sea of Galilee. A lot of people were around, and Jesus wanted some privacy with his disciples.

> Immediately Jesus made his disciples get into the boat and go on ahead of him to Bethsaida, while he dismissed the crowd. After leaving them, he went up on a mountainside to pray.
> When evening came, the boat was in the middle of the lake, and he was alone on land. He saw the disciples straining at the oars, because the wind was against them. About the fourth watch of the night he went out to them, walking on the lake. He was about to pass by them, but when they saw him walking on the lake, they thought he was a ghost. They cried out, because they all saw him and were terrified.
> Immediately he spoke to them and said, "Take courage! It is I. Don't be afraid." Then he climbed into the boat with them, and the wind died down. They were completely amazed, for they had not understood about the loaves; their hearts were hardened.

Jesus does all sorts of things in the Bible that are pretty amazing, things that only he can do—like walking on water all the way out to the middle of a big lake.

It would be nice if we could do that. We would never get our feet wet when we crossed a stream or even a puddle on the road. If you were swimming and you got a little tired, well, instead of swimming all the way back to the side of the pool, you could just climb up onto the water and walk back. Piece of cake.

All that would be nice, but every once in a while, we might want to show off a bit. Can you imagine if we could do some of the things Jesus did? We might want to use those powers to make us look important or to have people like us.

Jesus never showed off. He didn't do his miracles to impress people. Whenever he did any of his miracles, he was teaching people about who he was: the son of God. When he walked on the water, he was showing his disciples that the laws of nature did not control him—he controlled them, just like God.

The miracles of Jesus keep reminding us over and over again of this very important truth. Jesus has the same power over nature that God does—because he is God's son.

## Lesson 10

## Matthew 8:5–13

## A Soldier's Faith in Jesus

*What the Parent Should Know: A centurion is an officer in the Roman army who is in charge of 100 soldiers. (During Jesus' lifetime, the Romans were occupying Palestine.) The centurion is also a Gentile. Both of these facts set up the lesson being taught here in this episode.*

*The centurion's concern for his servant's illness prompts him to go to Jesus. Note, however, that the centurion doesn't actually ask Jesus to heal the servant. He just reports that the servant is paralyzed and suffering. But Jesus understands that the centurion wishes for his servant to be healed. And so he promises to come and heal him.*

*The centurion's response is "just say the word." Because the centurion is experienced in military matters, he understands the nature of authority: a commander says something and others simply do it. In the same way, Jesus' authority means that he simply says something, and it is done.*

*The response is well known to Christians, for it succinctly demonstrates the type of faith every Christian should have in Jesus. It does not mean that anything we ask of him he will do. It means that when we hand Jesus a problem, we turn it over to his authority. We leave it with him and do not need to check up periodically to make sure he hasn't forgotten.*

*Important, too, is the fact that the centurion is a Gentile. Jesus makes a point of elaborating on this, as he does so often in the Gospels. The centurion has the type of serene, unquestioning faith that God's chosen people, the Israelites, should be demonstrating at this very climactic moment, when the messiah is present among them. But they do not even come close. (It may help to understand that Matthew's Gospel is directed largely at Jews to persuade them to come to faith in Jesus as the messiah, and highlighting a Gentile's faith might prompt them to jealousy.)*

*We do not know how much the centurion understood about Jesus' ultimate identity. He probably did not understand how Jesus saw himself as the fulfillment of Israel's hopes. He certainly could not be expected to understand Israel's history and how Jesus fit into that history. And this is a central point in this story: as little as he knew compared with what the Jews should have known, he trusted Jesus to be able to heal his servant. And Jesus responded that the "subjects of the kingdom" (meaning the nation of Israel) would be left out of his kingdom, a kingdom where faith is the mark of inclusion, not ethnic identity.*

*That should not be understood in an unqualified way. Israel is not being "kicked out" of the kingdom. Instead, Jesus means that blessings will no longer come to a nation simply because it is a nation. Gentiles do not have to "become Jews." Rather, Gentiles can now be a part of "Israel," part of God's people, by trusting in Jesus—not by becoming ethnic Jews (for example, through circumcision, as we read in Galatians).*

*Begin by reading aloud:*

In today's story, Jesus is in the town of Capernaum. Capernaum was near the shore of the Sea of Galilee. The house of Jesus' disciple Peter was there, so it was a town where Jesus spent a lot of time.

In Capernaum, a centurion came to Jesus. At this time, the Romans were ruling Jesus' homeland, and a centurion was a Roman officer in charge of 100 Roman soldiers. ("Cent" comes from a Latin word that means 100. We use this word a lot today: it takes 100 *cents* to make a dollar. )

Here is the story from Matthew 8:

> When Jesus had entered Capernaum, a centurion came to him, asking for help. "Lord," he said, "my servant lies at home paralyzed and in terrible suffering."
>
> Jesus said to him, "I will go and heal him."
>
> The centurion replied, "Lord, I do not deserve to have you come under my roof. But just say the word, and my servant will be healed. For I myself am a man under authority, with soldiers under me. I tell this one, 'Go,' and he goes; and that one, 'Come,' and he comes. I say to my servant, 'Do this,' and he does it."
>
> When Jesus heard this, he was astonished and said to those following him, "I tell you the truth, I have not found anyone in Israel with such great faith. I say to you that many will come from the east and the west, and will take their places at the feast with Abraham, Isaac and Jacob in the kingdom of heaven. But the subjects of the kingdom will be thrown outside, into the darkness, where there will be weeping and gnashing of teeth."

Then Jesus said to the centurion, "Go! It will be done just as you believed it would." And his servant was healed at that very hour.

This centurion is a very kind man. He is concerned because his servant is very sick—the servant can't even move. The centurion wants Jesus to help the servant, so he walks right up to him and asks. Jesus says he will heal the servant, and that he will come right away.

But look at what the centurion says. "That won't be necessary, Jesus. You are a man like me. You have a lot of authority. Whatever you say happens right away. No need to come to my house. Just say so right now, and I know my servant will be healed."

The centurion showed so much faith in Jesus that even Jesus was surprised.

Now, think about when you are sick. You have a fever and your throat hurts, and you just feel tired and blah. You can't play or do school work. You don't even want to read or watch TV.

Your parents take you to the doctor. She looks at your throat, in your ears, takes your temperature, and says, "Yup, you have the flu. I'll give you some medicine. I want you to go home and drink a lot of fluids, and you have to stay in bed for one week. You'll feel better then."

The doctor gives you the medicine and you go home and rest. Soon you feel much better, because you did exactly what the doctor told you to do. You *trusted* the doctor when she told you what was wrong. You believed that she knew what she was talking about!

In the same way, the centurion trusted Jesus to heal the servant. He didn't say, "Hey Jesus, are you sure about that? Do you *really* know what you are doing? Are you *sure* you can make my servant better?" He believed right away that Jesus could and would heal his servant. No doubting!

# Unit 3

# Teachings of Jesus

For the Parent: Parables and miracles are teaching tools, but Jesus also taught the people in a more conventional manner that any first-century person would recognize, as a rabbi with a following. It is important, not only for children but all Christians, to see how much of Jesus' life was taken up by the double task of teaching the people about who God is and presenting God to the people through his actions.

Although few would put it this way deliberately, it seems to be a common assumption that the story of Jesus is mainly about a miraculous birth and his atoning death—with some filler material that bears indirectly somehow on what "the Gospel" is. But the teachings that Jesus gave to his disciples and others who came to hear him are more than filler. They are an expression of why he came in the first place.

Try this on for size: Jesus' teachings are every bit as much of the Gospel, the "good news," as any other part. In other words, the Gospel is more than just "getting saved." It includes this, of course, but Jesus' teachings about how we are to behave cannot be separated from "the Gospel." Otherwise, we sell short the grand vision of the Gospel and most of the Gospels will make little sense—not to mention the New Testament letters where Christian behavior is so often the topic of discussion.

# Matthew 19:13–15
## Jesus Blesses and Prays for the Children

*What the Parent Should Know: It is every Christian parent's comfort to know that Jesus blessed and prayed for children during his earthly ministry. In fact, he held children in such high esteem that he tells his disciples that his kingdom will be composed of "such as these" (v. 14).*

*As we have seen earlier, however, we should resist the temptation to think that the "kingdom of heaven" here means going to heaven, i.e, "you will not go to heaven unless you have a childlike faith." Rather, Jesus is referring to those who are willing to come to him and follow him in the here and now. Children are models of what it means to follow Jesus: a simple yet sincere trust.*

*It may help for adults to substitute the word "faith" with "trust." Often the two are interchangeable in the NT. Jesus certainly means more than an intellectual "belief," which is sometimes implied by the way we use the word "faith." Rather, we are confronted every day with a choice between "trust" or "fear."*

*To adults, Jesus is giving the command to trust him—as little children do so easily. Young children are eager to trust and rarely challenge or resist those whom they love unconditionally. Of course, any parent can attest to the times when children disobey, whine, etc. But young children are by and large trusting creatures who normally would never think that their loved ones would ever think of meaning them harm (and this innocence is violated in any form of child abuse).*

*This ability to trust is a gift children have, but it is all too quickly exchanged for an anxious existence. As children grow, they also need to be reminded of the advantages of childhood, which is precisely what Jesus is doing in this passage.*

*So children have a posture of trust toward Jesus. In return, Jesus' posture toward children is one of prayer and blessing.*

*Prayer and blessing are not the same. A prayer is speaking to God on behalf of others (or, of course, yourself). Blessing is speaking on behalf of God to someone else. The difference can be seen in some more liturgically minded churches. When the pastor prays on behalf of the people, his back is turned to the congregation and he is "facing God" on the altar. When he blesses, he is speaking for God and so turns toward the congregation. You might say that in praying for children and blessing them, Jesus has both bases covered.*

*Begin by reading aloud:*

> Then little children were brought to Jesus for him to place his hands on them and pray for them. But the disciples rebuked those who brought them.
>
> Jesus said, "Let the little children come to me, and do not hinder them, for the kingdom of heaven belongs to such as these." When he had placed his hands on them, he went on from there.

Parents brought their children to Jesus. He blessed the children and he prayed for them. Blessing and praying are a little bit alike, but not exactly the same. When you pray, you are *talking to God.* Praying for other people—talking to God about them—is something you do when you care about them and love them. When Jesus prays for the children, it shows us that he cares about children and loves them.

Think of a time when you prayed for someone. Maybe it was your mother or father, a brother or sister, a grandparent, a friend, or your pet. Maybe someone was sick or in trouble. You prayed for them because you cared about them and didn't want to see them hurt. Jesus prayed for the children because he cared for them.

Jesus also *blessed* the children. Blessing someone is different than praying for them. When you pray you usually fold your hands and talk to God. When you bless someone, you talk to a *person.* Instead of *folding* your hands, you put your hand on that person's *head*—at least that's how they did it in biblical times. You are not *asking* God for something. You are *telling* that person that God is with them and he loves them. That is what Jesus is telling the children.

The disciples thought Jesus was too busy for this, so they told the children to go away. But Jesus said, "No, let them come." Jesus blessed *and* prayed for the children who were brought to him. In this way, he shows us how much he cares for children.

But that isn't the only thing that we learn from this story. The children didn't say to their mothers and fathers, "No, I don't really trust this man. I don't want him to pray for me." They were not afraid of Jesus or suspicious. Instead they came to Jesus without any questions so that he could pray for them and bless them. This story tells us that grown-ups should be like children in this way. They should trust Jesus in the same way that these children did.

**Lesson 11: Jesus Blesses and Prays for the Children**

**Lesson 12**

# John 8:12

# Jesus Is the Light of the World

*What the Parent Should Know: This is one of seven "I am" statements found in John (the first is in 6:35, "I am the bread of life"). These sayings may appear very simple, almost childlike, but there is a lot going on here. The "I am" statements recall God's self-disclosure to Moses in Exodus 3:14 where he says, "I am who I am." In these statements, Jesus is making important claims to his own identity that echo this episode in Exodus.*

*There are two points being made in John 8:12. First, by claiming to be the light of the world, Jesus is making a strong claim about his own intimacy with the Father (see also John 8:16-19 below). This is similar to John 1:3–4, where Jesus is described as the one through whom all things exist and who is also the "light of men." By referring to himself as "light," Jesus is claiming a unique relationship with the Father.*

*Second, those who follow Jesus share in that light. This is similar to what Jesus says in Matthew 5:14, where the disciples are called the "light of the world." The light is not of their own making. It is a light that comes from their relationship to Jesus.*

*So, claiming to be the light of the world is a metaphor Jesus uses to under-line his claim to be sent by God and to be one with him. He is also claiming to be the source of light for his disciples as they follow him wherever they go and are "light" themselves. In other words, Jesus claims to be the mediator between God and humanity, a claim that does not sit well with the religious leaders of his day, as can be seen in verses 13 and following.*

*Begin by reading aloud:*

> When Jesus spoke again to the people, he said, "I am the light of the world. Whoever follows me will never walk in darkness, but will have the light of life."

Do you know that there are some places in the world where the sun is only up for a very short time during the day? For example, high up in the northern hemisphere, in the Arctic Circle, the nights are very long during the winter. In fact, one day each year, on the first day of winter, the sun does not come up at all.

Imagine if the sun never came up in the morning. That is hard to imagine, I know, because we see the sun every day. But try to imagine waking up in the morning when it is completely dark. And then imagine that it stays dark all day—through lunch and dinner. Then you go to bed and it is as dark as it was all day. The next day you wake up and do it all over again.

And it doesn't seem to end. You have to live like that day after day, week after week, month after month. Then, one day you wake up and there is your old friend the sun. Finally! Now you will be able to see without turning on a light or using a flashlight to play outside. And the snow will melt and it will begin to be warm again.

Jesus says he is the light of the world. Of course, he doesn't mean that he is a big sun up there in the sky. He means that before he came to the world, the world was "dark." That is an expression, a figure of speech—it is another way to say that "people did not really know God." When it is dark, you can't see where you are going or what you are doing. You also can't see what is going on around you. You just stumble around. This is what Jesus means about people who are not really able to under-stand who God is. They stumble around all their lives, not knowing what they're supposed to do, how they're supposed to think, or how to behave toward other people.

Jesus is like a light that makes the darkness go away. He is like the sun that comes up and makes everything day after it has been dark for many months. And Jesus promises that if we follow him—if we listen to what he says in the Bible—we will never stumble around in that darkness again. We will know God and learn more about how he wants us to think and act, every day.

| Lesson 13 | Matthew 8:18–22 |
|---|---|
| | Jesus Means Business |

*What the Parent Should Know: "Jesus meek and mild" is a common under-standing of Jesus' character. In some sense this is right: Jesus does give com-fort, forgiveness, love, acceptance. But following Jesus is a challenge as well. It is not always an experience of comfort, as any adult Christian can attest.*

*"Following" Jesus is an abstract concept for children, but it is still more concrete than saying "believing in Jesus." The Gospels are very dynamic, very action oriented, in describing what it means to be "connected" to Jesus. We sometimes think of this connection as a matter of the heart or mind, but the Gospels are adamant that actions and life habits are very much what Jesus is looking for in his disciples—not divorced from heart and mind, but a necessary result of what is in the heart and mind. This is not a matter of "salvation by works" but a clear indication that "following" Jesus involves more than just thinking and feeling.*

*In this passage, following Jesus involves a "cost." Following Jesus is not something to be taken lightly. It will result in the follower being as out of place as the one followed. It may also require the follower to put aside other duties in the interest of kingdom work. (Burying the dead was a very important Jewish duty at the time, and so Jesus here is saying that following him takes precedence over such customs—a very bold assertion.)*

*Jesus is no trendy leader looking for gullible groupies. He is building a kingdom, a way of living for God that the world does not recognize. Following this kind of leader is costly. (See Luke 14:25–35 where "the cost of being a disciple" is explained in more detail.)*

*The point here for children is not to scare them about how "tough" they need to be if they "really" want to be a Christian. Rather, as with so many of these lessons, the point here is to get to know the character of Jesus himself so that, when children are older, they will already have a maturing glimpse of the Jesus who is actually portrayed for us in the Gospels—not a caricature.*

*This Jesus is not trying to get people to like him and develop a fan base. He is holding out an invitation to those who would accept the challenge of living truly godly lives.*

*Begin by reading aloud:*

Jesus had just finished healing a lot of people near a lake called the Sea of Galilee. A large crowd had gathered around him. Some wanted to be healed, and others were just curious. Jesus was attracting a lot of attention.

Here is the story of what he did next:

> When Jesus saw the crowd around him, he gave orders to cross to the other side of the lake. Then a teacher of the law came to him and said, "Teacher, I will follow you wherever you go."
>
> Jesus replied, "Foxes have holes and birds of the air have nests, but the Son of Man has no place to lay his head."

Another disciple said to him, "Lord, first let me go and bury my father."

But Jesus told him, "Follow me, and let the dead bury their own dead."

There are all sorts of famous people in the world. There are movie stars and rock stars. They are on TV and in magazines. They are always having their picture taken, being driven around in limousines, going to important parties. A lot of people follow them all around. It is exciting to meet a famous person. We want to get his or her autograph, and tell our friends and family that we met someone who is on TV or in the movies. This can be a lot of fun.

Jesus was famous, too. Huge crowds followed him almost wherever he went, and some of them did this because they liked to be near a famous person. They liked the miracles that he did. Being near Jesus was exciting for them.

But Jesus isn't like a movie star who likes to get his picture taken. Jesus didn't want people to follow him just because everyone else was doing it. He didn't want followers who were only with him because he was famous. Jesus was teaching the people about God, and he wanted followers who were willing to listen to and try to understand what he had to say about God.

Sometimes, people who thought they wanted to follow Jesus grew angry when they actually listened to his teachings. Other stories in the Gospels tell us that when Jesus taught in synagogues, the leaders would order him to leave. (A synagogue was a place where the Jews of Jesus' day went to study and learn about God.) Some leaders even wanted Jesus to be killed. Jesus was famous, but he was not always welcome where he went—because his teachings were hard for people to understand and accept. His teachings made people angry. This is why Jesus says that even foxes have holes, but that he has no place to rest.

Jesus wanted the people around him to know that following him wasn't about excitement and fame. "If you are going to follow me," Jesus is saying, "don't always expect an easy time. It will be hard, too."

One person said, "I will follow you, Jesus, even though it might be hard, but first I have to bury my father." We don't know anything else about this man, but we can guess that his father had just died. In those days, if someone in your family died, it was your responsibility to bury them right away.

If this man didn't take care of his responsibilities, the rest of his family would be angry with him. The neighbors would gossip about what a bad son he was. They might ignore him when they met him in the street, or refuse to come to his house for dinner. Even though following Jesus would be the best thing this man could possibly do, it would make others angry and ruin his comfortable life.

This is what Jesus wanted his followers to understand. Being the fan of a famous person is fun—and easy, because you really don't have to do anything. But following Jesus is entirely different. Jesus is telling the people that if they want to become his disciples, their lives will not always be easy.

**Lesson 14**

## Matthew 11:28–30

## Jesus Gives Rest to the Weary

*What the Parent Should Know: This passage is one that is prone to some misunderstanding. It suggests a picture of Jesus who is warm, welcoming, and kind. This is all true, but the full impact of that picture can best be seen when we understand this passage is also a fierce criticism of the Pharisees, the religious leaders of the day.*

*Note how the passage is set up by vv. 25–27: "At that time Jesus said, 'I praise you, Father, Lord of heaven and earth, because you have hidden these things from the wise and learned, and revealed them to little children. Yes, Father, for this was your good pleasure. All things have been committed to me by my Father. No one knows the Son except the Father, and no one knows the Father except the Son and those to whom the Son chooses to reveal him.'"*

*Jesus is the conduit between God and humanity: only the Son knows the Father, and it is only through the Son that the Father can be known. So, knowing God is something that can only be done through knowing the Son.*

*This can only be fully understood if we remember that in Jesus' day it was through the study of Torah (the law given to Moses) that God's people would acquire wisdom and godliness. The "yoke" is a metaphor for the Law. It is something to be subject to, as a literal yoke was used to bind one ox to another for pulling a heavy load.*

*From an Old Testament perspective, this is certainly correct. The Law required a disciplined and determined lifestyle, but one that would reap great benefits for God's people (one need only skim the 176 verses of Psalm 119 to see this in action). But Jesus is saying, "I am now the yoke." He is replacing the Law as the means by which God's people know him; the people are now to learn from him, not teachers of the Law. To those who are burdened with the Law, namely those whose yoke is made excessive by the Pharisees, Jesus says "come to me . . . my yoke is easy . . . my burden is light." Jesus is gentle and humble, the very characteristics that will flourish in those who take his yoke upon them.*

*A yoke still implies a submission to something. Jesus' yoke is not a free ride, as if the actions of his followers don't matter ("Hey, get rid of the Law and follow me, we'll have a good time"). Rather it is a yoke of getting to know Jesus more and more, not the pressure of trying to be good enough for God.*

*This story complements the message of our last lesson. In that, Jesus was saying, "Don't think that following me is all fun and games." That message remains true, but we need to understand this aspect of following Jesus as well: Becoming his disciple also lifts a huge burden that is impossible for any of us to carry.*

*Begin by reading aloud:*

> "Come to me, all you who are weary and burdened, and I will give you rest. Take my yoke upon you and learn from me, for I am gentle and humble in heart, and you will find rest for your souls. For my yoke is easy and my burden is light."

Have you ever gone hiking or taken a long, long walk? Sometimes families like to go camping, and that usually involves a good bit of walking and carrying heavy backpacks.

That can be tiring. You wake up early in the morning, maybe before the sun even is up. You pack everything up—the tent, the food, the sleeping bags, bug spray, cooking pots, and who knows what else. And then, when you have put everything on your back and you begin walking, it doesn't take too long before you are exhausted.

In Jesus' day, many people were carrying around something else that was very heavy. But it wasn't a backpack.

Many people thought that, for God to love them, they had to be very careful to do all sorts of things *perfectly* so that God would not be angry. In Jesus' day, the way that the Jews learned about God was by studying the Law in the Old Testament. Sometimes this was just called "the Law."

Other times it was called "the Law of Moses." Another word you might have heard is "Torah." They all mean the same thing. The Law told the people what God is like and how to obey him. But following the Law was very hard work. And no one could do it completely right all the time.

In Jesus' day, the men who were supposed to teach people how to obey the Law were called Pharisees. But the Pharisees did not just teach their followers about the Law. They were so worried to make sure people kept the Law that they added extra laws. For example, the Old Testament says that you should not work on the Sabbath because that is a day of rest. But the Pharisees were afraid that people might work by accident and break the Law without knowing it. So they made all sorts of extra laws to keep people from even getting *close* to working on the Sabbath. They said that you couldn't carry anything on a journey, in case that might be working. They said that you couldn't gather food from a field if you were hungry. They even got angry with Jesus for healing someone on the Sabbath. Healing is a good thing to do, but the Pharisees said, "No, that is too much like work. We can't allow it."

It was hard to keep track of all that the Pharisees wanted the people to do. And it was even harder to do it right. Keeping track of all of the laws and following them all was like carrying a heavy burden on your back all the time. The word Jesus uses to describe this burden is "yoke." A yoke is a heavy wooden frame that joins together two animals so they can pull a heavy load, like two oxen pulling a wagon.

For the Jews of Jesus' time, studying the Law and obeying it was like having a yoke on you. Now, a yoke is not a bad thing at all. It keeps the oxen in line, working together, to get the job done. Having the Law as a "yoke" helped the people know how to live and know God. But Jesus was saying that the Pharisees made the yoke and the load they were pulling far, far too heavy by piling all those extra laws in the wagon. That heavy weight actually made it *harder* for the people to know God.

That is why Jesus tells the people to come to him. They are "weary" and "burdened" by this heavy weight placed on them by the Pharisees. But Jesus says they do not need to pull that burden. The only yoke they need is following Jesus and listening to him. That is why Jesus says, "Take *my yoke* upon you and learn from me." Jesus has a yoke, too, but his yoke will actually give the people *rest* from the heavy burden the Pharisees put on them.

Knowing God is not about having to keep a lot of laws in just the right way. Jesus is saying that knowing God is about following Jesus and listening to what he says.

# Luke 8:19–21

# Jesus' Mother and Brothers

*What the Parent Should Know: Jesus' ministry was a popular one, with crowds following him everywhere. In an age of security measures protecting our politicians, it is probably hard for us to grasp how easily accessible someone of Jesus' stature was in the ancient world.*

*In this story, Jesus isn't displaying disrespect or apathy toward his biological family (his mother, Mary, and his brothers, listed in Mark 6:3). It is true that his family really wanted to see him but were prevented by the crowd. After all, Jesus could have said to the crowd, "Can you give us a few minutes?" Instead, Jesus turns this into a lesson that is consistent with what he has been saying in the previous two parables in chapter 8 of Luke: the parable of the sower (8:1–15) and the parable of the lamp on a stand (8:16–18).*

*Both parables speak to the importance of hearing and doing. In the parable of the sower, three times the seed falls on harsh ground, not suited for growing, and so the plants do not flourish. All three soils represent those who only hear the word of God. It is only the seed that falls on "good soil," where the hearer "retains it" and perseveres (8:15), that yields a crop. In the same way, a lamp is not to be hidden, but put on a stand so that it actually gives off light. Having a lamp, i.e., "listening," is not enough. One must act.*

*In this passage about Jesus' mother and brothers, Jesus is not disparaging his biological family. Instead he is using the moment to emphasize how those who hear and do God's word are his "family." We have seen elsewhere (Lesson 10) that faith rather than ethnic identity is the mark of the kingdom of God. That faith is not simply an internal "belief" but a faith that is accompanied by a new pattern of living. And this is not limited to ethnic Israel, but open to all, Jew and Gentile. In both cases, being a part of Jesus' "family" is not determined by "biology" but an active faith.*

*Likewise, for us today, having an active faith—both believing and doing— is a mark of the intimate, familial relationship with him that we claim. We who put God's word into practice are his family (v. 21).*

*Begin by reading aloud:*

Now Jesus' mother and brothers came to see him, but they were not able to get near him because of the crowd. Someone told him, "Your mother and brothers are standing outside, wanting to see you."

He replied, "My mother and brothers are those who hear God's word and put it into practice."

Jesus spent a lot of time traveling around, telling people about God. He probably wasn't home very often. One day, Jesus' mother and brothers really wanted to see him, but there were so many people surrounding Jesus, they couldn't get close. Someone else had to tell Jesus they were there.

When he was told that his family wanted to see him, Jesus said something that sounds very strange to us. He didn't say, "Sure, let them through." He said, "My mother and brothers are those who *hear* what I have to say and then *do* it."

This does not mean that Jesus didn't love his family. He did. But Jesus used opportunities like this to teach something. He is saying here that those who follow him become his family. And to follow Jesus, to be his disciple, means to *listen* to what Jesus says, and then try to *behave* that way.

Sometimes a best friend can become like a member of your family— or you can feel like your best friend's family is *your* family. You can go to each other's houses and not feel like strangers. You can help yourself to food from the fridge, or play in your friend's yard, without even having to ask permission. You can spend the night at your friend's house, and he (or she) can spend the night at yours.

This is the sort of family that Jesus is talking about. He says that families are not just the people who are born related to each other. Families are people who love each other and decide to be with each other. Jesus is saying that all of his followers can be as close to him as his mother and his brothers. If they love him and follow what he says, they will become part of his family. And if we love and follow Jesus, *we* become part of his family as well.

# Unit 4

# The Sermon on the Mount

For the Parent: The Sermon on the Mount (Matthew 5–7) is really an extended example of Jesus' teachings (see previous unit). We are treating it as a separate unit, however, because it has some unique characteristics. First, Matthew's Gospel is very focused on presenting Jesus as a fulfillment of the Old Testament—not just in terms of a prophecy here and there, but rather in terms of the Old Testament as a whole finding its final meaning in Jesus. This is why, in the Sermon on the Mount, Matthew presents Jesus as a new and improved Moses, who is on a mountain giving a new "law" to the people. With every "you have heard it said . . . but I say to you" that Jesus utters, he is presenting himself as Israel's new deliverer, as someone who is giving the people a new law, a new Torah.

Second (and related), these teachings are a declaration of new "kingdom-behavior"—how the people of God are to act in his kingdom, with Jesus at its head. The Sermon on the Mount almost acts like a series of bylaws for the kingdom of heaven: "This is how my followers are to behave." In other words, they are not unrelated but interesting comments that take up space before the Gospels get to the important matters of Jesus' death and resurrection. They are the important matters that are given their final stamp of approval in Jesus' death and resurrection.

*What the Parent Should Know: Salt and light are two vivid images Jesus uses to describe the effect his followers should have on the world around them. In the days before refrigeration and electric light, these two elements were highly valued. Salt was both a preservative and used for flavoring. Oil lamps brought sustained light to the pitch blackness of ancient village life. Being salt and light means that our godly words and deeds bring light and life to an otherwise dark and bland existence, and by doing so, we show God to others. This is more than "good deeds." It is being like Jesus wherever we are.*

*The heart of this analogy, however, is a warning. Jesus' followers are salt and so are meant to exhibit an obvious and positive effect wherever they are. But that salt can lose its saltiness. Jesus does not elaborate on how this can happen, but the result is that, when salt ceases being salt, it is discarded. Again, Jesus does not tell us what precisely this means, but he is not talking about "losing your salvation." That is pressing the analogy too far. Salt is simply a metaphor for what his followers are supposed to be like in the world around them, and a failure to do so makes them unfit for kingdom work.*

*Likewise, followers of Jesus are light, and he tells them not to restrict the natural effects of light. A city on a hill or a light on a stand is the first thing you notice in an otherwise dark place. This is what light does. One has to make an extra effort to make light work contrary to its natural properties: one must put the light under a bowl in order to conceal it.*

*It should be stressed that this teaching follows upon the sayings known as the Beatitudes (5:1–12). The types of behaviors described there, with all their benefits (seeing God, possessing the kingdom of heaven, etc.), are the very things that characterize the saltiness and light of kingdom living.*

*If you think it might be helpful, you can review the "light of the world" story in Lesson 12 before continuing.*

*Begin by reading aloud:*

> "You are the salt of the earth. But if the salt loses its saltiness, how can it be made salty again? It is no longer good for anything, except to be thrown out and trampled by men.

"You are the light of the world. A city on a hill cannot be hidden. Neither do people light a lamp and put it under a bowl. Instead they put it on its stand, and it gives light to everyone in the house. In the same way, let your light shine before men, that they may see your good deeds and praise your Father in heaven."

Jesus talks here about salt and light. We have already read one story in which Jesus says that he is the "light of the world." That means that Jesus is the bright light that lets people see God more clearly. In this passage, Jesus is talking about light again, but this time it is his disciples who are not only light but also salt.

Let's think about light and salt for a minute. Have you ever walked into your house at night when it is pitch dark? That can be very scary. The first thing you want to do is turn on the light so the house can be bright and you won't be scared anymore.

When you put salt on your food, it tastes so much better. Can you imagine potato chips without any salt? That wouldn't taste good at all. Also, before there were refrigerators, salt was used to keep food from spoiling. If you've ever seen meat that was left out on the kitchen counter for a day or two, you'll know how important it is to keep food from spoiling. Meat left out without salt or refrigeration starts to smell and taste absolutely horrible.

Jesus is using stories about light and salt to explain what it means to follow him. Salt and light were very important in Jesus' day. Without salt, there was no way of preserving food, especially meat. If you slaughtered a cow, for example, you needed salt to keep the meat from going bad. If you didn't have salt you either had to eat all the meat right away, or eat some and let the rest of it rot. And the people of Jesus' day needed lamps every single evening so that they wouldn't stumble around in the dark. In modern times we have light wherever we go. In fact, there is so much light coming from large cities that it is impossible to see the stars in the night sky. But in Jesus' day, there were no electric lights. Every night, it became so pitch black that no one could see. Without lamps and torches, the whole world fell into complete darkness every night.

Everyone back then understood how salt kept food from rotting and how light made a dark place bright and inviting. Jesus wants his followers to be like salt and light.

In the next few lessons, you will learn about some ways that Jesus wants his followers to behave. In this part of the Gospel of Matthew, Jesus is talking about the kingdom of God, and about the new ways in which his followers—the people who belong to the kingdom of God—are supposed to act.

When you learn about these new ways to behave and begin to do them, you become like salt and light. Even if everyone around you is acting in rotten and spoiled ways, you can be different—and perhaps the people who see you behaving in Jesus' new way will see you, and begin to understand what it means to be different. Maybe they will begin to see what Jesus is like. In this story, Jesus is telling his followers to remember that they bring Jesus' teaching with them, wherever they go. Through their actions, everyone around them can see for themselves what God is really like.

**Lesson 17**

**Matthew 5:33–37**

# Just Be Truthful

*What the Parent Should Know: In the Old Testament, the making and swearing of oaths was a well-documented practice. One can catch a glimpse of this practice in such places as Genesis 21:22–24; 26:26–33; Numbers 30:2; Deuteronomy 6:13–14; 10:20; 23:21–23; Leviticus 19:12; Ecclesiastes 5:4–6. The purpose of an oath was to insure the truthfulness of someone's word by calling upon God. Hence, we read of swearing "by God's name" or similar phrases.*

*Swearing by God's name meant calling upon God to be both a witness to the promise made in the oath and a judge against the oath taker if he did not follow through. Of course, this is serious business, for taking an oath in God's name but not following through amounts to breaking the Third Commandment, i.e., taking the Lord's name in vain. This means more than just "cursing" in the modern sense—it implies disrespect for God's name as well.*

*Also, swearing an oath in God's name was for serious matters, such as politics (see the Genesis passages above) as well as issues pertaining to the proper treatment of fellow Israelites. It was not a casual or everyday thing to do. By contrast, think of how flippantly "swear to God" is used in contemporary culture.*

*Oaths were actually established by God himself. For example, Deuteronomy 10:20: "Fear the Lord your God and serve him. Hold fast to him* and take oaths in his name." But what then are we to make of Jesus' words in Matthew 5:33–37? Does he not contrast the swearing of an oath "long ago" (in the Old Testament) with a different command for what he now says people should do? Long ago they swore oaths, "But I tell you, do not swear at all" (v. 34).

There are two things at work here. On the one hand, there is a clear sense in which Jesus is laying aside the entire Old Testament practice of taking oaths in God's name. This is what v. 34 implies. On the other hand, Jesus' focus in the verses that follow is not so much on oaths in general, but in swearing "by" something other than God, namely heaven, Jerusalem, or one's "head" (life). What is going on with that?

In Jesus' day, the swearing of oaths was common practice, but there was a reticence about swearing by God's name, for the reason stated above: the possibility of misusing God's name if the oath could not be kept. By swearing by something less than God's name, be it heaven, earth, Jerusalem, or one's own life (see James 5:12 for a near parallel of Matthew 5:33–37), one could still make an oath but have a loophole waiting in case things didn't work out.

This is the primary situation into which Jesus is speaking, and the modern example is a pinky swear or crossing your fingers when making a promise. You can sound sincere but leave yourself an out if you want to. In other words, the making of oaths had become so corrupted that Jesus says to his listeners: leave the practice behind entirely. A new kingdom ethic is at work that moves beyond all of that. The oath taker who is a member of the kingdom of God does not need to swear at all, even by God's name (as sanctioned in the Old Testament).

This brief passage is actually somewhat involved, but a general principle comes through nonetheless. A true follower of Jesus speaks plainly and does not need to support his or her words by an appeal to something outside of him- or herself. Rather than giving one's words the stamp of reliability, as it did in the Old Testament, swearing an oath of any sort in the new kingdom era actually detracts from that reliability. Things are different. The true guarantee of reliable speech is an inner transformation by the Spirit of Christ, not an outward act.

Jesus puts it in stark terms. The person who legitimizes his words with an oath is demonstrating that he is not really following Jesus. He is not really displaying the kind of kingdom ethics Jesus is preaching in the Sermon on the Mount. He is leaving himself an "out." This is why Jesus says at the end that anything more than a simple Yes or No is ultimately "from the evil one" (v. 37). That doesn't mean that the words are demonic, but that such oaths oppose the kingdom that Jesus is building.

**Lesson 17: Just Be Truthful**

*Begin by reading aloud:*

"Again, you have heard that it was said to the people long ago, 'Do not break your oath, but keep the oaths you have made to the Lord.' But I tell you, Do not swear at all: either by heaven, for it is God's throne; or by the earth, for it is his footstool; or by Jerusalem, for it is the city of the Great King. And do not swear by your head, for you cannot make even one hair white or black. Simply let your 'Yes' be 'Yes,' and your 'No,' 'No'; anything beyond this comes from the evil one."

Jesus is teaching the people something new here. That is why he begins with "You have heard that it was said . . . long ago." "Long ago" means that Jesus is talking about old customs that the Jews still followed.

In the Old Testament, people made promises to show that they were telling the truth. The Bible calls this an oath. Today, when a new president is elected, he stands in front of the whole country on TV and takes an "oath of office," which means he is promising to be a good and faithful president.

To show that they were serious about a promise, the Israelites would take an oath by swearing by God's name. That meant they were making the promise not only to other people, but to God, too. That was very serious, and not keeping the promise would be sinning against God. Even today in some courtrooms, witnesses put their hands on a Bible and say "I promise to tell the truth, the whole truth, and nothing but the truth, *so help me God.*" That is an oath in God's name

In Jesus' day, people still made oaths, but they were getting a bit sneaky about it. Instead of taking an oath in God's name, they would take an oath by something else. Jesus mentioned four of these other ways: heaven, earth, Jerusalem, and one's "head" (which means one's own life). This was like a pinky promise or a "fingers-crossed" promise. It was a way of making a promise—but if you wanted to break the promise, you could do it because you had only made it to another person, and not to God at all. What started as a good thing, to make a promise in God's name in the Old Testament, had been changed so that people could get out of honoring the oath.

But Jesus says that, no matter what kind of an oath you make, when you break it you are still being dishonest. You can't swear by heaven to get out of keeping your promise, because heaven is where God is. Earth is his "footstool" (where kings sitting on their throne rest their feet).

Lesson 17: Just Be Truthful

Heaven is where God's throne is so you still have to keep your promise. You can't swear by Jerusalem either. Jerusalem is God's city, where the Great King rules. (The Great King is a way of talking about God.) And you can't swear by your life ("by your head") because it is an empty promise: you can't really control your life. If you swear by any of these things, you are still bound to keep your promise!

Using an oath to keep a promise had gotten to be a big problem in Jesus' time, so Jesus just says, "Forget the whole thing. No more oaths at all." Now there is a new way of loving God and doing what he says. We are to be truthful in all we say. That is what Jesus means when he says "Simply let your 'Yes' be 'Yes,' and your "No,' 'No.'" There is no need to add anything like "I swear" or "cross my heart." Truthful people don't *need* to add things like that to let others know that they are really telling the truth. And because we are followers of Jesus, we are called to be truthful.

# Lesson 18

# Matthew 5:38–42
# An Eye for an Eye, A Tooth for a Tooth

*What the Parent Should Know: Old Testament law teaches that the punishment for a serious injury must be paid for in kind (Exodus 21:23–25; Leviticus 24:19–20; Deuteronomy 19:21). The purpose of these laws is that the punishment must fit the crime—no more and no less. The laws were certainly not meant to encourage vengeance, as it might appear to the naked eye, but to do the exact opposite: to make sure that no more punishment was exacted than what the crime deserved.*

*In this passage, Jesus is unmistakably referring to this Old Testament law, but as we see so often in the Sermon on the Mount, he is now bringing a bigger picture to bear, the picture of the kingdom of heaven (or of God).*

*The Old Testament law pertains to matters of civil law, where people in positions of authority have a right to enforce the law. In other words, Israel's law was for the adminstration of a nation, to make sure that justice was served. "Eye for an eye" is not a "lower" form of morality—particularly in the ancient world where the abuse of the powerless and common people was a frequent problem. It was a way of establishing a fairer set of laws for judges and administrators to use.*

*Jesus, however, is concerned with how we react personally. He wants to make clear that no one should claim this Old Testament law (meant for the use of a nation) as an excuse for personal vengeance. Jesus' kingdom ethic is clear: on a personal level you answer injustice with love.*

*We have seen before that Matthew's Gospel is especially concerned to portray Jesus as a second Moses, a new lawgiver. Jesus here is establishing his authority as greater than that of Moses. He is saying, "I am here now. This is a new 'law' under which we are now to live."*

*The "new law" that Jesus is establishing here is one of humility and servanthood toward others. This new law should replace our tendency to think first of how we can legitimately retaliate if we are harmed. (By the way, the "evil person" Jesus refers to in v. 39 means simply the person who inflicts the harm, the perpetrator. That is how "evil" is used often in the Bible. It is not a description of someone's overall character or his general state of sinfulness.) Note that Jesus is saying something more than simply "make sure you keep the Old Testament law properly." He is saying that the law itself needs reconsideration in view of the kingdom ethic of personal responsibility and morality.*

*Children can quickly grasp the radical nature of this message. It is only natural to want to retaliate for personal injury. Every child understands that instinctively. Jesus also understands this, but teaches that we should not follow our natural instincts. In fact, we should go out of our way to serve others, even those who mean us harm. Of course, we are dealing with children here, whereas Jesus is talking to adults. Children are in naturally vulnerable positions, and (obviously) should not be taught to turn the other cheek to abuse or to let a bully have his way. Hence, the examples below are all "safe" examples concerning people not normally expected to harm children (siblings and friends). Of course, parents should feel at complete liberty to adjust this lesson to address specific concerns.*

*Begin by reading aloud:*

> "You have heard that it was said, 'Eye for eye, and tooth for tooth.' But I tell you, Do not resist an evil person. If someone strikes you on the right cheek, turn to him the other also. And if someone wants to sue you and take your tunic, let him have your cloak as well. If someone forces you to go one mile, go with him two miles. Give to the one who asks you, and do not turn away from the one who wants to borrow from you."

In the Old Testament, God gave the Israelites laws to make sure they treated each other fairly. So if one person hurt another, the punishment

Lesson 18: An Eye for an Eye, A Tooth for a Tooth

given by the judges would have to be fair. This is what "eye for eye, and tooth for tooth" means. The punishment has to be fair. The punishment has to "fit the crime," which is how we put it today. If someone broke a small law, they should receive a small punishment. You don't put someone in jail for twenty years for running a red light! The laws in the Old Testament were meant to make sure that small crimes were given small punishments.

But Jesus is saying something different here. Some people in his day were using these laws to get even with those who did unkind, or thoughtless, or even evil things to them. Instead of asking judges to help them, the people who were offended took matters into their own hands and did the exact same thing back. But these laws were meant for judges and rulers to use, not for the people. If someone steals your family car, what do your parents do? They call the police. Later there is a trial and the judge decides on the punishment. Your parents don't chase the thief down, take their car back, and then steal the thief's car!

Jesus wants the people to understand this—and he wants them to know something even more important. He is telling his followers, "When you are treated unfairly, don't try to get even. I know that it feels right to get even. I understand. Still, don't do anything at all to get back at someone who does an unkind thing to you. In fact, if they are unkind to you, you should be even more kind to them. That is the new way of doing things in the kingdom of God. That is how you show others what God's love is like."

Have you ever been on the floor playing with a toy, and your brother or someone comes over, pushes you out of the way, and takes the toy and starts playing with it? Or maybe someone comes into the living room and changes the channel on the TV while you are watching your favorite show? Or maybe another child does something really nasty like punch you because he isn't getting his way?

Jesus is saying we should not try to get back at unkind people by doing something unkind ourselves. Instead, we should do something that takes a lot of bravery. Jesus is saying something that is very important and very hard to do sometimes. "Don't fight back."

When someone takes something from us or pushes us or says something mean, we often want to get back at them. That is normal. Everyone feels that way. We want to grab them, take the toy out of their hand, and yell? "HEY, THAT'S MINE!" When your brother or sister pushes you down to get something from you, you want to push back and yell, "HEY, CUT THAT OUT!!" And then a big fight starts with a lot of yelling and screaming and maybe even some pushing and punching.

**Lesson 18: An Eye for an Eye, A Tooth for a Tooth**

Jesus understands this, but he wants his people to do something that is very different, and also difficult. If someone grabs a toy out of your hand, instead of yelling and fighting, give him *another* toy. Or if someone barges in and changes the channel on the TV, say, "OK, let's watch what you want to watch."

Yes, sometimes you need to tell your parents or teacher when people are unkind or harm you in some way. When you are a child and someone does something unkind to you, it's often a very good thing to tell a teacher or parent what is going on. Jesus is saying that when people do mean things to us, we should not fight back *ourselves*. It takes two people to fight, two people to get into an argument, two people to yell at each other. Jesus is saying "Be the person who walks away from a fight—and does something kind instead."

**Lesson 19**

**Matthew 6:25–34**

**One Day at a Time**

*What the Parent Should Know: It is hard to think of a more timely teaching of Jesus for contemporary Western society. As I write this, the world is in the midst of a severe economic downturn. Unemployment is up, people are losing their houses, the future is uncertain, and people are afraid.*

*Jesus' words here, however, are not an easy remedy. If you stop to think about it, saying that we should "not worry" about basic necessities by saying "look at the birds and lilies" is nonsensical. Birds and lilies have nothing to worry about: one is an animal without the capacity for abstract thought, and the other a fully non-thinking plant. By definition they HAVE nothing to worry about. A more relevant comparison might have been with the faithful neighbor down the street who does not worry, for God supplies all his needs. "God will take care of you, too," would be understandable.*

*But don't be fooled. Jesus' choice of object lessons is penetrating and disarming. The fact that birds and plants have, by definition, nothing to worry about is precisely Jesus' point. To those who have learned that their true treasure is in heaven, that they actually cannot serve two masters (vv. 19–24), worry is out of the question. For these people, worry is as impossible for them as it is for birds and plants. It simply doesn't exist.*

*It is those who do not trust God, the "pagans" of v. 32, who run after these things. But for followers of Christ, we are to "seek first his kingdom and his righteousness." This does not mean having your head in the clouds, waiting for heaven and blissful existence. It means living each day, not thinking about food and clothing, but where your first priority is living in such a way that reflects the teaching of Jesus, the kingdom he is building, his righteousness.*

*Six-year-olds do not have the same capacity for worry about basic necessities as adults. They can, however, begin to develop a mental picture of what it means to follow Jesus: we trust God to supply our needs so our energies can be devoted to kingdom living, i.e., acting and thinking in ways that suit a follower of Jesus.*

*Begin by reading aloud:*

> "Therefore I tell you, do not worry about your life, what you will eat or drink; or about your body, what you will wear. Is not life more important than food, and the body more important than clothes? Look at the birds of the air; they do not sow or reap or store away in barns, and yet your heavenly Father feeds them. Are you not much more valuable than they? Who of you by worrying can add a single hour to his life?
>
> "And why do you worry about clothes? See how the lilies of the field grow. They do not labor or spin. Yet I tell you that not even Solomon in all his splendor was dressed like one of these. If that is how God clothes the grass of the field, which is here today and tomorrow is thrown into the fire, will he not much more clothe you, O you of little faith? So do not worry, saying, 'What shall we eat?' or 'What shall we drink?' or 'What shall we wear?' For the pagans run after all these things, and your heavenly Father knows that you need them. But seek first his kingdom and his righteousness, and all these things will be given to you as well.
>
> "Therefore do not worry about tomorrow, for tomorrow will worry about itself. Each day has enough trouble of its own."

Are you wearing clothes right now? Of course you are! (What a silly question.) Did you eat something today? You probably did. If you didn't yet, you probably will very soon.

Who gave you your clothes? Probably a grown-up gave them to you or bought them from a store. How did all that food get into your house? Probably an adult went to the grocery store and bought it for you.

When you are out playing or watching TV, you don't think to yourself, "Oh no! Where am I going to get some clothes to wear when I wake up tomorrow?" or "I have no idea how I am going to eat breakfast when I get up tomorrow!" You don't worry about those things because they will all be right there waiting for you. Someone else takes care of it for you every day.

In this story, Jesus is saying something just like that. He is telling his followers that it is not their job to worry constantly about whether they will have enough food or clothing in the future. Instead, it is their job to think about how they can continue to follow him.

This is hard for grown-ups to do—and when you get older, you will probably find it hard to do as well. But right now, you can understand what Jesus means by this teaching, probably better than the grown-ups around you. You can think about what it means to be kind to those who do unkind things to you, without worrying about whether you'll get any dinner. You can work, every day, on speaking the truth, instead of concentrating on finding clothes to wear tomorrow.

This is what Jesus is saying to his people. He is saying, "Put your energy where it belongs. Work hard to understand what it means to follow me—instead of worrying constantly about what the future will bring." Often, when Jesus is teaching, he tells his followers that they should "be like children." This is one of the times when children find it easier to understand what Jesus means than grown-ups do!

## Lesson 20

## Matthew 7:7–12

## You Can Ask God Anything

*What the Parent Should Know: This passage can be thought of in two parts, vv. 7–11 and v. 12. It may look like v. 12 (the "Golden Rule") is just tacked on, but that is not the case.*

*As for the first part, Jesus is making a point in a way that he employs elsewhere: "If even x is true, how much more do you think y is true?" Incidentally, this type of argumentation is a common one among rabbis, and is called in Hebrew "qal va-homer," or in English "easy and hard." If the hard things can be done, how much more can the easy things be done? (In contemporary* logic, this is known by the Latin term a fortiori) So in this case, "if even a father treats his son well, how much more do your think your heavenly Father will treat you well?" Jesus uses the concrete to illustrate the abstract, as he typically does.

It is assumed here that followers of Jesus will indeed ask, seek, and knock. This implies persistence, but not in the sense of the "persistent widow" story he tells elsewhere (Lesson 2, Luke 18:1–8). Rather, the picture painted here is of a father who will be quick to answer the door and satisfy the seeker.

What does Jesus mean in describing his hearers as "evil" in v. 11? It is tempting to see here an echo of original sin and the fallenness of all of humanity, but this is more likely a rhetorical device on Jesus' part to express the strong contrast between God's whole goodness and the human penchant for corruption and mistreatment of others. Words like "evil" and "righteous" have a broader range of meanings than we sometimes give them. Here "evil" is not so much a deep theological declaration as it is a practical observation. People tend to wrong each other. Human beings can't be counted on to be fair and just. But even human beings know how to treat their children. So why in the world would someone doubt that God would be immune to our requests?

The second part, v. 12, calls upon the disciples to put into practice what they see the Father doing to them. In the same way that the Father gives "good gifts to all who ask," Jesus' followers should be eager to mete out the same generosity to others. This is why Jesus' version of the Golden Rule is proactive: not "don't do what you don't want done to you," but "do to others."

Such behavior (amazingly, when you stop to think about it), "sums up the Law and the Prophets." A proactive show of love toward others is nothing less than a summation of biblical (Old Testament) teaching. "Law" means not just laws, but the entire Pentateuch. "Prophets" does not just mean the prophetic books, but in addition some of what we call the "Historical Books" (Joshua, Judges, 1 and 2 Samuel, and 1 and 2 Kings). It is true in a certain sense that reading so much of the Old Testament can be a chore indeed, and much of it seems so irrelevant. But here, we see Jesus' own declaration as to the heart of what the Old Testament is about. By acting toward others the way God acts toward us, we have entered the center of God's will as expressed in the Old Testament.

Begin by reading aloud:

> "Ask and it will be given to you; seek and you will find; knock and the door will be opened to you. For everyone who asks receives; he who seeks finds; and to him who knocks, the door will be opened.

"Which of you, if his son asks for bread, will give him a stone? Or if he asks for a fish, will give him a snake? If you, then, though you are evil, know how to give good gifts to your children, how much more will your Father in heaven give good gifts to those who ask him! So in everything, do to others what you would have them do to you, for this sums up the Law and the Prophets."

God can seem far away to us. That is because we cannot see him, like you can see your parents, or hear him, like you can hear the grown-ups you trust to take care of you.

It is easy to trust someone that you can see or hear. If you ask your father or mother for something that you need, don't they give it to you? What if you have grown out of all of your clothes and you need new ones? Maybe they won't buy you all the clothes you want or the most expensive clothes. But they probably don't dress you in a big garbage bag or wrap you in aluminum foil either. Your parents know how to take care of you. If you are hungry, don't your parents feed you? At dinner time, they don't let you go hungry, and they don't give you a shoe to eat, do they?

But parents are not perfect. They make mistakes, just like everyone else. Sometimes parents can be in a bad mood. They might speak sharply to you, or blame you for something you didn't mean to do, because they are tired or feeling sick or just plain busy. This is what Jesus means when he calls parents "evil." He doesn't mean they are evil in the same way that monsters or villains are evil. He means that *all* people are imperfect, and *no one* is as good as God.

Now, if your imperfect parents are able to love you so much that they take care of you, you can be sure your *heavenly* father will care for you, too. That doesn't mean that your parents don't really love you. They do. It means that God loves you more than even your own parents.

Jesus isn't saying that God will give us *everything* we want. He knows that we sometimes want things we shouldn't have. But Jesus *is* saying that you should expect God to be kind to you, even more kind than your imperfect parents can be.

And this is why Jesus says "do to others what you would have them do to you." Jesus wants his followers to be kind to other people just as God is kind to them. If someone comes to you and asks *you* for help or needs you to do a favor, you should be kind to them, too. That doesn't mean you do *anything* someone asks you ("Hey, can you help me lie to my mother?"). It just means that you should be ready to be kind to people you know—just as God is ready to be kind to you.

Jesus is serious about this. He is saying that when we love others around us, no matter what, we are doing exactly what God has wanted his people to do all along. We are behaving to others just as God behaves toward us. This is what he means when he says "this sums up the Law and the Prophets." "Law and Prophets" was a way of saying "the Old Testament." (They didn't call it "the Old Testament" back then.) When you show others the kindness that God has shown you, you are doing what the Bible has been commanding all along.

# Unit 5

# Jesus' Early Life

For the Parent: There are essentially three phases to Jesus' life as presented in the Gospels: the early years before his ministry begins (which is the topic of this unit), his ministry years (where there is a steady movement from general acceptance to rejection of Jesus' message), and the end of his life (Passion Week). The stories of Jesus' early life are much more involved than our Christmas pageants might suggest. They are theologically loaded statements about who Jesus is, connecting him to Israel's story in the Old Testament (as can be seen most clearly in the genealogies of Matthew and Luke), and foreshadowing much of what is to follow in the Gospels. In other words, they are not a sort of picture album of Jesus' boyhood ("Oh, and here's the time the little guy wandered away from his parents.") They are setting up the story of Jesus, and so demand our attention.

Like the other units dealing with Jesus' life, this one does not try to cover every detail. Instead, certain themes are highlighted. The assumption is that this curriculum is not the student's only exposure to the basic outline of Jesus' life and ministry.

# Lesson 21

## Matthew 1:18–25

## Jesus' Birth

*What the Parent Should Know: The story of Jesus' birth is well known to even casual readers of the Bible. Joseph and Mary are pledged to be married. This is anything but a casual relationship! Before their marriage, Joseph finds Mary to be pregnant, and so has "in mind to divorce her quietly" (Matthew 1:19). The pledged relationship was so binding that a legal divorce was required to sever it. Joseph's motive for doing this quietly was to avoid the penalty of stoning for Mary.*

*But Joseph found out through angelic visitation that Mary was pregnant by the Holy Spirit (note that only Luke describes the angelic announcement to Mary; Luke 1:26–38). This episode, which receives very little elaboration, is the moment of the incarnation, the conception of the God-man (the Latin root means "to make flesh"). The incarnation is perhaps the single most difficult concept for any Christian to grasp. In fact, the early church did not reach a general agreement on how to think of the incarnation until the Council of Chalecedon in A.D. 451, and even afterward the history of the church is marked by arguments over different ways to explain this most mysterious of Christian doctrines.*

*It is also curious that only Matthew and Luke mention the moment of incarnation. The other Gospels are silent, as is the rest of the New Testament. Matthew's decision to highlight the unique nature of Jesus' birth is no doubt connected to his Jewish audience. Matthew, who presents Jesus to his readers as Israel's messiah, is consistent in making connections between the story of Jesus and the Old Testament.*

*In 1:22–23, Matthew cites Isaiah 7:14 to connect Jesus' birth with Israel's story. A glance at the context: Isaiah is referring to an attack on Jerusalem, ruled by King Ahaz of Judah, by a coalition of hostile forces. Isaiah assures King Ahaz that God will side with Jerusalem and Judah, and God gives him a sign. A child will be born, and before that child is old enough to "choose the right and reject the wrong" the coalition will be dissolved and "laid waste" (see especially Isaiah 7:16–17). This child will be called, symbolically, "Immanuel," which means "God with us," which is exactly what happened in Ahaz's day: God was with Judah, and the particular child born during the time of Ahaz was the sign.*

*But Matthew, as he often does, is arguing that the ultimate fulfillment of the Old Testament is actually far beyond what the Old Testament prophets themselves understood. The full significance of their words would not be understood until Jesus himself came. The "child" as a sign of "God with us" receives its fullest expression in Jesus' birth.*

*The incarnation is difficult to explain, even for experienced theologians— and it is doubly difficult to explain to children. For this reason, this lesson will focus not on the conception or other complexities of this passage, but on the purpose of Jesus' birth: this was God's way of being with his people.*

*Begin by reading aloud:*

Before we read today's story, I want to explain two words to you. "Christ" and "messiah" are two words that both mean "anointed one." An "anointed one" is specially chosen by God. In the Old Testament, when God chose a man to be king, that man was "anointed"—he had special oil poured on his head to show that God had picked him for a particular job. You will hear "Christ" and "messiah" both used to describe Jesus.

Now listen to this story:

> This is how the birth of Jesus Christ came about: His mother Mary was pledged to be married to Joseph, but before they came together, she was found to be with child through the Holy Spirit. Because Joseph her husband was a righteous man and did not want to expose her to public disgrace, he had in mind to divorce her quietly.
>
> But after he had considered this, an angel of the Lord appeared to him in a dream and said, "Joseph son of David, do not be afraid to take Mary home as your wife, because what is conceived in her is from the Holy Spirit. She will give birth to a son, and you are to give him the name Jesus, because he will save his people from their sins."
>
> All this took place to fulfill what the Lord had said through the prophet: "The virgin will be with child and will give birth to a son, and they will call him Immanuel"—which means, "God with us."
>
> When Joseph woke up, he did what the angel of the Lord had commanded him and took Mary home as his wife. But he had no union with her until she gave birth to a son. And he gave him the name Jesus.

At the beginning of this story, Joseph and Mary were not yet married. Couples were only supposed to have children *after* they were married—so Joseph was surprised and disappointed to find out that Mary was going to have a baby. The law at that time said that Joseph could call off the marriage. Today, it is only a married couple that gets a divorce. But back then, being engaged was a serious promise to get married. You couldn't just break up; the law said that you had to get a divorce to call off the wedding.

The law also said that if a woman who was not yet married became pregnant, she could be stoned to death. But Joseph was a good man. He wanted to divorce Mary quietly so that she would not be punished.

Joseph did not yet understand that Mary had not done anything wrong. Mary was going to have a baby because of a miracle God did. Mary was going to have the baby—but the child came from God.

Why did God do this? Because he wanted to live on earth like us, to be with us. That is what the word "Immanuel" means: God with us.

God knows what it is like to be you or me. God *made* us, but he also knows what it is like to *be* us. He did this because he loves us.

We sometimes think of God with a white beard, sitting far away up in heaven. That is just make-believe. No one can describe what God is like. That's why he became a man, Jesus, so people could see face to face what God is like. Jesus came to explain to us who God is.

Imagine that you are promised a bicycle for your birthday. You are excited, and you ask your parents what it looks like. They describe it to you, and you can sort of imagine it, but it's just not real to you. You're disappointed, because you are excited but the bicycle is only something in your mind. Then your parents say, "Tell you what. Rather than describing the bike, what if we just *show* it to you?" They wheel it out from the garage and you see it—with all its colors, shiny chrome, gears, and brakes. That's better than just thinking about it. Now you really *know* what the bike is like.

God came to earth to be like us so that we would really *know* what he was like. But there is a second purpose in God's coming to earth. Because God became human, he knows, just like you do, how it feels to be happy, sad, afraid, lonely, sick, and every other way we might feel. When he tells us things like "love your enemy" he knows how hard it can be to do that. When he says "obey your mother and father" he understands that sometimes you may be frustrated and not want to obey. When he says "do not be afraid," he understands just what it means to be afraid—really afraid.

God became a person to show us that he loves us—and that is who Jesus is.

# God Protects Jesus from the King

*What the Parent Should Know: Matthew's Gospel is the only one to record this well-known episode of the Magi. "Magi" is best understood as referring to a class of people who were known for reading the stars. This was a commonly accepted practice in antiquity, considered a source of wisdom, which is why we traditionally refer to the Magi as "wise men." The tradition of "three" wise men is based on the fact that three types of gifts were brought (gold, frankincense, and myrrh). Matthew neither states how many there were, nor their names (although tradition refers to them as Balthasar, Caspar, and Melchior).*

*This story highlights a couple of things. First, it shows that distant, eastern stargazers were more attuned to the birth of Jesus than was the reigning King of Judea, Herod (actually a non-Jew, an Idumean, native to the area which now belongs to Jordan), who was appointed to his post by the Romans. Second, it shows the very serious level of political opposition against Jesus from the very beginning. This characterizes all four Gospels.*

*For Herod, the ancient prophecy of Micah (cited in v. 6) is a threat to his rule rather than a source of rejoicing, as it is for the eastern wise men. So Herod, the most powerful man in Israel, seeks to destroy the child, and it is only through God's intervention in a dream that the Magi are warned not to return to Herod.*

*This episode in Jesus' life is very similar to the infant Moses' narrow escape from Pharaoh's decree (Exodus 2:1–10). As we have already seen, there are other parts of Matthew's Gospel where Matthew presents Jesus as a kind of Moses. For example, the Sermon on the Mount (Matthew 5–7) shows Jesus on a mountain as a new lawgiver of sorts. Matthew's purpose is to reveal that Jesus is a new and better Moses, worthy of Jewish allegiance.*

*The focus of this lesson is on God's deliverance of the peasant infant Jesus, despite the intrigue of the most powerful man in the kingdom. The point of this for children is not a moral lesson, such as, "God will always come to your rescue." The story simply helps children appreciate something about Jesus' early life that is not always emphasized: the extent to which Jesus was opposed throughout his life by the powers of the day.*

*Begin by reading aloud:*

After Jesus was born in Bethlehem in Judea, during the time of King Herod, Magi from the east came to Jerusalem and asked, "Where is the one who has been born king of the Jews? We saw his star in the east and have come to worship him."

When King Herod heard this he was disturbed, and all Jerusalem with him. When he had called together all the people's chief priests and teachers of the law, he asked them where the Christ was to be born. "In Bethlehem in Judea," they replied, "for this is what the prophet has written: 'But you, Bethlehem, in the land of Judah, are by no means least among the rulers of Judah; for out of you will come a ruler who will be the shepherd of my people Israel.'"

Then Herod called the Magi secretly and found out from them the exact time the star had appeared. He sent them to Bethlehem and said, "Go and make a careful search for the child. As soon as you find him, report to me, so that I too may go and worship him."

After they had heard the king, they went on their way, and the star they had seen in the east went ahead of them until it stopped over the place where the child was. When they saw the star, they were overjoyed. On coming to the house, they saw the child with his mother Mary, and they bowed down and worshiped him. Then they opened their treasures and presented him with gifts of gold and of incense and of myrrh. And having been warned in a dream not to go back to Herod, they returned to their country by another route.

This story tells us that Magi—men who studied the stars—came from far away in the east to see Jesus at his birth. The Magi knew he was to be born because they saw his star. Back then, looking at the stars was something that only very wise, very educated people did. Studying the stars was a way of learning what was happening in the world.

These wise men came from far away to see a baby being born, because they knew that this was not an ordinary child. They knew that this baby was to become king of the Jews.

You might think this news would make everyone happy, but it didn't. When Jesus was born, the Jews already had a king—King Herod. When the wise men came to King Herod asking where the new king was, King Herod was frightened. You can imagine how he felt! Many people hated Herod, and if there was another king, somewhere in his country, Herod could lose his throne—especially if his subjects liked the other king better.

**Lesson 22: God Protects Jesus from the King**

Herod did not want anyone taking his power away. *He* was king of the Jews, and no little baby was going to change that. Even though Jesus was just very small, Herod wanted to kill him.

This would not be the last time that a leader disliked Jesus. All through Jesus' life, rulers were against him. They did not always like what Jesus said. Sometimes kings and rulers thought that Jesus wanted to take over, and so they wanted to stop him. Sometimes priests and teachers were criticized by Jesus, and so they wanted to kill him. Many powerful people throughout Jesus' entire life were against him, starting when he was a baby.

But God made sure that Jesus would be protected. He warned the wise men in a dream not to go back to Herod. Even the most powerful man in the kingdom, King Herod, could not destroy Jesus, no matter how hard he tried. Even though rulers and other powerful people on earth opposed Jesus, God's power protected him.

| Lesson | Matthew 2:13–15 |
|---|---|
| **23** | Jesus' Life Is in Danger |

*What the Parent Should Know: After the Magi left Jesus and returned to their country (having been warned in a dream not to go back to Herod— Matthew 2:12), an angel came to Joseph and told him the same thing: keep away from Herod. So Joseph took Mary and Jesus (still an infant but of undetermined age) to Egypt.*

*This flight to Egypt is patterned after the Old Testament. Both Abraham (Genesis 12:10–20) and later the Israelites (under Jacob) fled to Egypt for safety. In those cases they were escaping a famine, whereas Jesus suffered under a different type of hard circumstance. This is another way in which Matthew portrays Jesus as being connected with the Old Testament.*

*Matthew also cites two Old Testament prophecies to further establish the connection between Jesus and Israel's story in the Old Testament: Hosea 11:1 and Jeremiah 31:15. The flight to Egypt was predicted, according to Matthew, by Hosea, although here, too, there is more of a "pattern" involved than a direct prophecy. Hosea was not thinking about Jesus going to Egypt as a boy. He was talking about the nation of Israel. By citing Hosea, Matthew* is saying that Jesus' whole life, even as an infant, reflects Israel's destiny. He is the "new Israel."

The central thrust of the passage, as with the previous passage about the Magi, is that Jesus' life was in danger from the beginning by a ruthless and callous man, one who was also the most powerful man in Jesus' life. But God was more powerful still.

Note that this lesson does not go beyond v. 15. The slaughter of the innocent children (vv. 16–18) is something that cannot be addressed with first graders. We feel this story is too difficult for children to comprehend in a constructive manner. However, parents can appreciate the tension this episode causes. There is an all-out assault on Jesus by the most powerful man in the kingdom, which further supports the theme of Jesus' threat to the powerful. Also, the slaughter of the male infants is another connection with the Exodus story, where the male infants are thrown into the Nile (Exodus 1:20–22) out of fear that the Israelites would otherwise grow too many and rebel. The citation of Jeremiah 31:15 is not immediately clear, but Matthew's intention is similar to what we saw above with Isaiah 7: Matthew is connecting an episode in Jesus' life with an episode in Israel's story, thus shouting to his readers "Jesus fulfills Israel's story."

Begin by reading aloud:

> When they had gone, an angel of the Lord appeared to Joseph in a dream. "Get up," he said, "take the child and his mother and escape to Egypt. Stay there until I tell you, for Herod is going to search for the child to kill him."
>
> So he got up, took the child and his mother during the night and left for Egypt, where he stayed until the death of Herod. And so was fulfilled what the Lord had said through the prophet: "Out of Egypt I called my son."

Herod was not at all happy about the baby that people claimed was the king of the Jews. Herod was the king of the Jews, and he liked it that way. He did not want a baby growing up in his kingdom who might one day take his power away from him.

And Herod had the power to get rid of Jesus. In fact, Herod could do pretty much anything he wanted to the people under his rule. That is the way things were back then.

Today, many countries have elections where the people decide what leader they want ruling them. Many countries also have laws that even the rulers have to follow. The president of the United States holds the

Lesson 23: Jesus' Life Is in Danger

highest office in the country, but he cannot do whatever he wants. He has laws to follow, just like everyone else.

But Herod did not have to follow laws. He was powerful and he could do what he wanted. No human being could stand in his way. Even Herod could not defy God, though. God protected the life of Jesus because Jesus had not yet begun the job he came to do.

This story of Jesus as a baby is a lot like what happened to the Israelites in the Old Testament. The Israelites went down into Egypt to escape something very bad in their own country—a famine in the land, during which all the crops died. They were afraid that they would starve, so they went to Egypt, where there was food. While the Israelites were living in Egypt, the Egyptians made them into slaves. They lived as slaves for a long time, until God called Moses to lead the Israelites out of slavery in Egypt and back to their own land.

This is what is happening with Jesus, too. Jesus and his family had to escape something dangerous in their own country—an evil king who meant to harm Jesus. They went down into Egypt in order to be safe. But Jesus and his parents would not stay in Egypt. In the next lesson, we will read about how God called Jesus up out of Egypt back to his land.

It isn't just a coincidence that Jesus and the Israelites both went down to Egypt and then came home again. Both stories show us that evil cannot destroy God's plans for his people. Neither a horrible famine nor a wicked king could get in the way of what God intends. God is more powerful than nature—and far more powerful than the evil intentions of any man.

Lesson
24

Matthew 2:19–23
Jesus and His Family
Come Back Home

*What the Parent Should Know: Once again, an angel appears to Joseph with a message, this time calling him to return home. As we have seen in the previous lessons, Matthew models Jesus after Moses, who likewise returns to his homeland (Egypt) after the threat to take his life has subsided. In Matthew 2:20, Matthew even borrows the language used in the Old Testament to describe Moses' return: "for all the men who wanted to kill you are dead"*

*(Exodus 4:19). Both Moses and Jesus need to return to their homeland in order to continue with the task of delivering their people.*

*Jesus' return, however, would not be to the territory of Judea (where Bethlehem was). Herod's son, Archelaus, was now in charge, and this was too much of a risk. So Joseph took his family instead to the district of Galilee, in the north. Their new home would be Nazareth.*

*Matthew refers to this move as fulfilling a prophecy (v. 23), but there is no Old Testament prophecy like this. Matthew is likely making a deeper and more subtle theological point here. Calling someone a "Nazarene" in Jesus' day was like calling someone a hillbilly. The Old Testament speaks of Israel's messiah as being "despised" (e.g., Isaiah 53:3), and so Matthew drew a connection between Jesus' new town and what the Old Testament in general (not a specific verse) said about the messiah. "Nazarene" may also be connected to the Hebrew word for "branch" (netser). Since the messiah will be a "branch" or "a shoot from the stump of Jesse" (Isaiah 11:1), coming from that town would have helped establish Jesus' credentials. Both of these possible explanations are speculative, since Matthew doesn't actually say what he is thinking here.*

*At any rate, Matthew is very intent to present Jesus to his readers as deeply connected to Israel's story in the Old Testament—as we have already seen in the previous lessons from Jesus' childhood.*

*Begin by reading aloud:*

> After Herod died, an angel of the Lord appeared in a dream to Joseph in Egypt and said, "Get up, take the child and his mother and go to the land of Israel, for those who were trying to take the child's life are dead."
>
> So he got up, took the child and his mother and went to the land of Israel. But when he heard that Archelaus was reigning in Judea in place of his father Herod, he was afraid to go there. Having been warned in a dream, he withdrew to the district of Galilee, and he went and lived in a town called Nazareth. So was fulfilled what was said through the prophets: "He will be called a Nazarene."

This is another story Matthew tells about Jesus' life as a small child. We have already seen that the Magi from the east came a great distance to see Jesus, because they knew he was a king. We also saw that this made Herod very angry, so that he wanted to kill Jesus. That's why Jesus's family took him far away, all the way to Egypt—to get away from Herod.

But now, King Herod was dead and it was safe for the family to go back home. So they packed up and began the long journey out of Egypt.

They didn't go back to Bethlehem, though. There was another evil king there now. His name was Archelaus, and he was Herod's son. So an angel warned Joseph to go to a town called Nazareth in an area called Galilee.

Nazareth was a very small town. It wasn't an important city, like Jerusalem or Bethlehem. Important and powerful people did not live there. So why did the angel tell them to go to Nazareth? Jesus was born a king. Why did the angel tell a king to go to such a little town and not to a bigger, more exciting city?

Jesus was a king, but not like the other kings. He did not live in a big palace in a big city. He did not wear expensive clothes and have servants doing things for him. Jesus was a humble king, not a proud king. A king like Jesus needed to grow up in a small town, a town that people would not think was important, a town they might not even know was there. Jesus had to live in a place like Nazareth.

We can also see here that Jesus' life is a lot like Moses'. Moses grew up in Egypt, but then he left his home because the Pharaoh wanted to kill him. He fled to the desert and lived there until that Pharaoh had died. Jesus also fled from a harsh king and came back home after that king was dead.

Moses and Jesus have a lot in common. Both fled an evil king, returned after that king died, and then delivered the people from danger. The difference between Moses and Jesus is that Moses delivered the people from slavery and brought them to the Promised Land (Israel). Jesus delivered his people from their sin and made them members of his kingdom.

# Unit 6

# Jesus' Disciples

For the Parent: The identity of Jesus' disciples, and the types of exchanges Jesus had with them, give us yet another angle from which to understand who Jesus was and what he did. The fact that there were twelve disciples is not random, but a clear echo of the twelve tribes of Israel. The very fact that Jesus had disciples at all is itself a theological statement: Jesus is starting up a "new Israel," the kingdom of God/heaven, although this one will ultimately be made up of Jews and Gentiles and will not be founded on the Mosaic law. One might say that the disciples were the first citizens of this new kingdom. This whole notion of Jesus and the new Israel follows nicely on the previous lessons on Jesus' early life, where Matthew especially makes this very point—that Jesus is bringing a new kingdom, a new "version," as it were, of Israel.

It is also encouraging to us to see the extent to which Jesus' closest followers simply keep missing the point of his words and actions. Jesus' message, although very much tied to Israel's story in the Old Testament, was also fresh and to a certain extent unexpected. It had to be taught patiently, over a three-year period of Jesus' public ministry, and was not given its clearest expression until Easter and Pentecost. If even Jesus' hand-picked disciples required such an extended education to catch on, we should not be surprised if the message of Jesus sometimes requires effort on our part to comprehend.

# Lesson 25

## Jesus' First Disciples

*What the Parent Should Know: The calling of the first disciples is a well-known story, in part because of the memorable catchphrase of making fishermen into "fishers of men." The first disciples were two sets of brothers, all occupied with their daily chores when Jesus came to them. First called were Simon Peter and Andrew, then James and John, sons of Zebedee.*

*The story is told with no fanfare, and the focus seems to be on the immediacy with which they left their work behind and followed Jesus. No explanation is given, and readers throughout the centuries have been left to ponder what might have driven these men to make an apparently precipitous, risky move. What was it about Jesus that made them act so? Was it the work of the Spirit, moving them in unexpected ways? The immediate and unconditional nature of their response is meant to signal, early on in the Gospel story, the gravity and power of Jesus and his mission.*

*Begin by reading aloud:*

> As Jesus was walking beside the Sea of Galilee, he saw two brothers, Simon called Peter and his brother Andrew. They were casting a net into the lake, for they were fishermen. "Come, follow me," Jesus said, "and I will make you fishers of men." At once they left their nets and followed him.
>
> Going on from there, he saw two other brothers, James son of Zebedee and his brother John. They were in a boat with their father Zebedee, preparing their nets. Jesus called them, and immediately they left the boat and their father and followed him.

Have you and your friends ever gone on a field trip to the zoo with your parents or teachers? The grown-ups who are with you say, "Stay close to me, children. Go wherever I go. Do whatever I do. Stay with me." And wherever they go, you go. Otherwise you might get lost.

As you walk through the zoo, your parents or teachers tell you about the animals. You learn their names, where they come from, what they eat, when they sleep, and all sorts of interesting things.

Jesus was a teacher, too. Jesus had friends who followed him wherever he went. They are called his disciples. The disciples followed Jesus all over, listened to him, and learned from him.

In this story we see that Jesus' first disciples were fishermen. Their names were Simon, his brother Andrew, and then James and his brother John. Before they began to follow Jesus, they were very busy with their nets. If they did not catch enough fish they would be hungry. But when Jesus told them to stop what they were doing and follow him, they did—right away.

If you think about it for a minute, that is not something you see every day. Think of a road crew—the people who use jackhammers and backhoes and other tools to dig up the road and fix the pipes underground. Like fishermen, they work very hard. Imagine that they are in the middle of a big project. They've dug huge holes, the road is all torn up, and cars are all backed up and can't get through. Then someone comes along—not a boss, but someone they have never seen before—and says, "Stop what you are doing right now and follow me."

This person doesn't explain anything. He doesn't tell them his name or what he wants. He just says, "I want you to come with me."

What do you think the road workers would do? They would probably ignore the stranger, or think he was crazy. But the disciples didn't do that. When Jesus called them, they stopped right away and went with him.

The story doesn't tell us what they were thinking, or why they decided to go and follow. But they must have looked at Jesus and realized that there was something different about him. They must have known that God was with him—and so they were willing to drop everything and follow him.

**Lesson 26**

**Matthew 9:9–13**

## Jesus Is a Friend of the Shunned

*What the Parent Should Know: Tax collectors in Jesus' day were held in great disdain by the general population. Not only did they collect taxes from the Jews to give to their hated captors, the Romans, they also overtaxed and* kept the extra for themselves. So they were both traitors and extortionists. The people who were victimized had no means of seeking justice, so hatred for the tax collectors was strong.

For Jesus to enter the town of Capernaum (see 9:1) and walk up to a tax collector and say "follow me" was risky business. If Jesus wanted to secure a following that would give him credibility among his compatriots, this was not the way to do it. In fact, as we see in v. 10, Jesus later has dinner with a house full of these "tax collectors and sinners," which gets people talking. This is not what holy men, teachers of Israel, should be doing. It would be like a politician today, whose campaign was moving in the right direction, meeting up with known crooked stock traders at a restaurant—and recruiting some of them for his staff.

But here, once again, Jesus shows how his calling is different from—diametrically opposed to—cultural expectations. By calling Matthew to follow him, Jesus demonstrates in concrete terms what his calling is. He is not here to befriend the righteous, but sinners. In doing so, Jesus fulfills the Old Testament ideal of showing mercy toward those in need of help (he cites Hosea 6:6 in vv. 12–13). The quote is not a throwaway line. Jesus, by calling people like Matthew to follow him, is showing mercy to as despised a group of people as existed. In this way, he was fulfilling the messianic pattern of the Old Testament.

We should pause for a moment to consider the use of the words "righteous" and "sinner." Jesus uses these words as they were used in the Old Testament and understood in his own day: both of these terms have to do with behavior, doing what is right or what is wrong in God's eyes. So when Jesus says he has not come to call the righteous, he does not mean people who are self-righteous, nor is he describing merely an inner spiritual state (as it is often understood by Christians today). He is referring to whether or not someone lives a life in submission to God's standard of conduct.

The focus of this lesson is on Jesus' relentless commitment to reach those who are farthest away from God. For Paul (in Romans, for example), all of humanity is sinful and falls short of the mark. But Jesus' focus here is slightly different. He is speaking to fellow Jews and telling them he has come to bring everyone up to speed, rather than write off the scum and surround himself only with "the good."

Begin by reading aloud:

At the beginning of this story, Jesus has returned to the town of Capernaum. He has just finished healing a sick man and is walking back through the streets when he sees a very unpopular man ahead of him. Here is what happens next:

> As Jesus went on from there, he saw a man named Matthew sitting at the tax collector's booth. "Follow me," he told him, and Matthew got up and followed him.
>
> While Jesus was having dinner at Matthew's house, many tax collectors and "sinners" came and ate with him and his disciples. When the Pharisees saw this, they asked his disciples, "Why does your teacher eat with tax collectors and 'sinners'?"
>
> On hearing this, Jesus said, "It is not the healthy who need a doctor, but the sick. But go and learn what this means: 'I desire mercy, not sacrifice.' For I have not come to call the righteous, but sinners."

You know what a bully is: someone who's bigger and meaner than you and uses that to make your life miserable. A neighborhood bully might pick on younger children who walk by his house. A school bully might try to knock a smaller child's tray out of his hands at lunch, or steal his papers and books just to get him in trouble. If there's a bully around, most people try to stay away. They hope that if they leave the bully alone, he'll leave *them* alone.

In Jesus' day, tax collectors were sort of like bullies. The tax collectors were supposed to make people give up some of their money, so that the money could go to a king no one liked. That was bad enough, but the tax collectors also took *more* taxes from the people than they were supposed to. Then they kept the extra for themselves.

People hated these tax collectors and wanted to keep as far away from them as they could. But look at what Jesus does instead. He makes friends with the tax collector named Matthew. Then he goes to Matthew's house to have dinner with him and all the other tax collectors.

The other people who live in the town are horrified to see Jesus with the tax collectors. After all, these tax collectors are *enemies!* They are wicked and dishonest—and they try to hurt others.

But Jesus says, "The bullies are the ones who *really* need to know what God is like. They need me more than anyone else. The people who are the farthest away from God are the ones I came to rescue."

# John 1:43–51

# Philip and Nathanael

*What the Parent Should Know: In Lesson 25 we looked at the first disciples Jesus called: Andrew, Simon, James, and John. The calling of Philip and Nathanael is told only in John's Gospel (John does not mention James and John). Like the first four men, Philip responds immediately.*

*But Nathanael is incredulous at the messiah coming from Nazareth. The town was of no significance (see Lesson 24). When Nathanael expresses his doubts, Philip gets him to come see Jesus for himself (see also 1:39). As Nathanael approaches, Jesus comments at how there is nothing "false" in Nathanael, which simply means that he is a good, decent fellow who is straight up and direct, as we see in his honest comment to Philip in v. 46.*

*The heart of this passage is in how Jesus knew Nathanael before Nathanael ever made the effort to come to know him. Jesus saw him sitting under the fig tree before Nathanael ever thought to "come and see." This is one of the great paradoxes of the faith: we come to Jesus only to realize that Jesus knows us before we know him.*

*This realization brought Nathanael to confess Jesus as rabbi (authoritative teacher) and Son of God/King of Israel. These latter two titles are interchangeable in this context. "Son of God" can mean several things in the Old Testament, including humanity in general, but it also refers to the ideal king, David (2 Samuel 7:14; Psalm 2:7; 89:27). Nathanael is not making a declaration of Jesus' divinity but of his kingship.*

*Jesus rewards Nathanael's faith by assuring him that he will see even greater things, namely "heaven open and the angels ascending and descending on the Son of Man." "Son of Man" is a favorite term Jesus uses to designate himself. Although the term typically simply means "human" (or more simply, "I"), in this context Jesus likely has Daniel 7:13–14 in mind, which was understood in his day to refer to a messianic figure. The ascending/descending issue refers to Jacob's ladder (Genesis 28:12). By alluding to this Old Testament episode, Jesus is saying two things: that he is the new Jacob—or better, the new Israel (since Jacob's name was Israel), and that his disciples will come to see plainly that heaven itself will bear witness to that.*

*This is a packed passage. Jesus is Rabbi, King, and Israel all wrapped up into one. And he also saw Nathanael before Nathanael knew him. For the purposes of introducing this story to young children, we will focus on this last part.*

*Begin by reading aloud:*

The next day Jesus decided to leave for Galilee. Finding Philip, he said to him, "Follow me."

Philip, like Andrew and Peter, was from the town of Bethsaida. Philip found Nathanael and told him, "We have found the one Moses wrote about in the Law, and about whom the prophets also wrote—Jesus of Nazareth, the son of Joseph."

"Nazareth! Can anything good come from there?" Nathanael asked.

"Come and see," said Philip.

When Jesus saw Nathanael approaching, he said of him, "Here is a true Israelite, in whom there is nothing false."

"How do you know me?" Nathanael asked.

Jesus answered, "I saw you while you were still under the fig tree before Philip called you."

Then Nathanael declared, "Rabbi, you are the Son of God; you are the King of Israel."

Jesus said, "You believe because I told you I saw you under the fig tree. You shall see greater things than that." He then added, "I tell you the truth, you shall see heaven open, and the angels of God ascending and descending on the Son of Man."

In this story, Jesus calls another disciple to follow him—Philip. Philip then runs to tell his friend Nathanael that he has met the messiah—the anointed one, the king that the prophets said would come. But Nathanael doesn't believe him. Someone as important as the messiah would not come from such a little town as Nazareth. Important people come from important places.

But Nathanael went to meet Jesus anyway. Can you imagine his surprise when he met Jesus and learned that Jesus already knew him, before Nathanael ever came to meet him?

Think about that for a second. Nathanael goes with his friend to see this Jesus, to check him out to see if he is as important as Philip says. I don't think Nathanael was expecting to find anyone all that interesting. So as he is coming, Jesus says, "Ah, I see that you are a good man." Nathanael wonders how in the world this man Jesus could know anything about him. But Jesus says more. He tells Nathanael that even before

Philip came to get him, Jesus already knew who he was. Nathanael is astonished by this! He says, "Jesus, you really are the great teacher and the great king, and I will follow you and be your disciple."

Jesus knew Nathanael before Nathanael met Jesus. And the great thing is that Jesus knows not just Nathanael but all of his followers like that. That includes you, too. You know Jesus, but do you realize that he knew you long before you even thought of him? Jesus has been thinking of you and bringing you to himself all along.

## Lesson 28

## Luke 10:38–42

# A Story of Two Sisters

*What the Parent Should Know: This short story about Martha and Mary seems like a random episode, just thrown in at some point in Luke's Gospel (it does not appear in the other Gospels). It is, however, another story about discipleship and what it means to follow Jesus. Note how this story is sandwiched between the parable of the Good Samaritan and Jesus' teaching about prayer, both of which challenge Jesus' audience to move beyond conventional ways of thinking. There is more to this episode than meets the eye.*

*In this story, we find Jesus at the house of Martha and Mary, having been invited by the former while Jesus and his disciples were in town (Bethany; see John 12:1–3). Martha prepares a meal for her guests, an honorable activity, particularly in the ancient world where hospitality was highly valued. But she is not too happy that her sister Mary is sitting around listening to Jesus rather than helping.*

*On one level, Martha is correct to have some feelings about this. It is Mary's house, too, and it is her obligation, particularly as a woman in the ancient world, to serve the guests. One could certainly envision the man of the household going off in deep conversation with his male guests while others took care of the meal, but we would not expect a woman to do the same thing. In Jesus' day, women were not particularly worthy of "sitting in on classes," so to speak. They did not receive instruction from religious teachers.*

*But here we have a woman sitting at Jesus feet. This may be a bit subtle for our contemporary sensibilities, but we see here a woman so eager to hear Jesus that she obliterates custom—and Jesus commends her for it.*

*On another level, we see Martha's misstep, not that she was preoccupied with meal preparation (she was right to do so), but that she was preoccupied with what her sister was doing. When following Jesus, one should not be too quick in casting judgment on other followers. This is not a blanket endorsement to "do whatever and never take correction." Rather, it is a reminder that followers of Jesus may not always be at the same place in their journey. What Martha was doing was good, but she would have done better simply to keep serving and maybe even to rejoice a bit that her sister had a chance to sit at Jesus' feet for an evening. Both were doing what they needed to, and had Martha not judged her sister, she would not have received Jesus' gentle rebuke.*

*This entire episode is reminiscent of a recurring theme in* The Chronicles of Narnia *by C. S. Lewis. Whenever any of the children question Aslan about any of the other children—whether just out of idle curiosity or to see if everyone is being treated fairly by Aslan—he says more or less the same thing: mind your own business; their story is theirs, yours is yours.*

*Begin by reading aloud:*

> As Jesus and his disciples were on their way, he came to a village where a woman named Martha opened her home to him. She had a sister called Mary, who sat at the Lord's feet listening to what he said. But Martha was distracted by all the preparations that had to be made. She came to him and asked, "Lord, don't you care that my sister has left me to do the work by myself? Tell her to help me!"
>
> "Martha, Martha," the Lord answered, "you are worried and upset about many things, but only one thing is needed. Mary has chosen what is better, and it will not be taken away from her."

This is the story of two sisters and what happens when Jesus comes to their house for dinner.

In Jesus' day, showing hospitality was very important. There were no hotels or restaurants for people who were traveling. If you wanted to eat or sleep during a journey, you had to rely on the kindness of others. This is what happened here. Jesus and his disciples were passing through town, and Martha invited them over for a meal.

The problem, though, was that Martha was busy getting dinner ready while her sister Mary was sitting around listening to Jesus. Mary didn't help at all. Martha got upset and complained: it wasn't fair that she had to do all the work!

Martha isn't doing anything wrong by preparing the dinner. Someone has to cook the food! But neither is Mary doing anything wrong. In fact, Jesus even tells Martha, "Mary has chosen what is better." We can imagine what Mary is thinking: Jesus is here and we'll probably never get another chance to sit and listen to him talk!

Jesus is saying that both sisters are right. Both of them have chosen to do something important. If Martha had not complained, Jesus wouldn't have said anything to her. She would have gone on cooking and being hospitable, and Mary would have gone on listening. Both of the sisters would have been doing a good thing.

But Martha did something wrong. She did not mind her own business. She thought Mary needed to be doing what *Martha* wanted done. She did not think that maybe it was right for Mary to be doing something else. She did not realize that BOTH she and her sister were serving Jesus—but each in her own way.

God knows that all of us serve him differently, too. He gives each of us different abilities and different tasks to do. For example, in church, some people serve God by cooking the meal for the Sunday lunch. Others serve God by being in front of people and leading the singing. Both are serving God the way they think is right. Both are doing something important. There is no need for one to be jealous of the other, the way Martha was.

**Lesson 28: A Story of Two Sisters**

# Unit 7

# Opposition to Jesus

For the Parent: As anyone who has read the Gospels can see, Jesus' words and actions were met with considerable resistance, particularly by the religious leaders of the day, and to a lesser extent by the political leaders (especially at the end of his life).

But this was to be expected. A noted New Testament scholar puts it this way: if you knew nothing of Christianity and had never heard of Jesus, but you did understand something of the delicate religious and political situation of first-century Palestine, and then you opened up the Gospels and began reading, it would not be long before you stopped and asked, "How long will it take before this Jesus guy gets himself killed?" Jesus' ministry met with considerable opposition because he challenged rigid, blindly traditional understandings of God and the Old Testament as well as the ultimate supremacy of Rome's status as "world power." To the Jewish authorities, Jesus said, "If you know me, you know Yahweh. He sent me." To the Romans he said, "Caesar is OK as far as he goes, but your ultimate allegiance is to the true God, whom I represent."

There is much to be learned about Jesus by paying close attention to his interactions with his opponents. By seeing how Jesus responded to his adversaries, we catch a glimpse from a different angle of how Jesus understood his task on earth. Jesus reveals something of himself in the midst of these debates and struggles.

# Jesus Is Tempted

*What the Parent Should Know: The three-fold temptation of Jesus is a very serious matter. We must keep in mind that for it to be called a "temptation" it had to be a real temptation. This was no slam-dunk, perfunctory thing. The temptation was real and the stakes were high. In other words, there was a true possibility of giving in to temptation, otherwise it wouldn't be a real temptation. Would Jesus' entire mission, his messianic call, be derailed at the very beginning?*

*Here at the outset of Jesus' public ministry, he meets the most formidable of foes, the devil (v. 1., a.k.a. the tempter, v. 3), who has at his disposal the means to carry through on his promises to Jesus. We hear a faint echo of the Garden of Eden, where temptation was not resisted. But here we see Jesus, the new Adam (see Romans 5:14 and 1 Corinthians 15:22) who is tempted yet obedient (Hebrews 4:15).*

*Another Old Testament echo is found in v. 2. The forty days and nights echoes the familiar Old Testament pattern seen with Moses' time on Mount Sinai (Exodus 24:18; 34:28) and Elijah's flight to Horeb (i.e., Sinai; 1 Kings 19:8). More importantly, it echoes Israel's forty years of wilderness wandering which, according to Deuteronomy 8:2–3, was Israel's period of "testing."*

*We learn here what kind of messiah Jesus is resolved to be: one whose only goal is to accomplish the Father's will. He will not use his divine power for self-preservation (v. 4); he will trust God rather than test the intimacy of their relationship (v. 7); he will worship God rather than make any compromise with the devil (v. 10).*

*The primary lesson to be learned is not so much "be like Jesus" but "Jesus can be trusted." His messiahship is secure, and Jesus will not be deterred.*

*Begin by reading aloud:*

> Then Jesus was led by the Spirit into the wilderness to be tempted by the devil. After fasting forty days and forty nights, he was hungry. The tempter came to him and said, "If you are the Son of God, tell these stones to become bread." Jesus answered, "It is written: 'Man does not live on bread alone, but on every word that comes from the mouth of God.'"
>
> Then the devil took him to the holy city and had him stand on the highest point of the temple. "If you are the Son of God," he said, "throw yourself down.

For it is written: 'He will command his angels concerning you, and they will lift you up in their hands, so that you will not strike your foot against a stone.'"

Jesus answered him, "It is also written: 'Do not put the Lord your God to the test.'"

Again, the devil took him to a very high mountain and showed him all the kingdoms of the world and their splendor. "All this I will give you," he said, "if you will bow down and worship me."

Jesus said to him, "Away from me, Satan! For it is written: 'Worship the Lord your God, and serve him only.'"

Then the devil left him, and angels came and attended him.

God sent Jesus to earth for a very important reason: to show people what God is like. This is what Jesus talked about all the time. And everything he did during his years on earth, like helping the poor and healing the sick, showed people what God is like.

But the devil is God's enemy. In other parts of the Bible, he is called the evil one, or the tempter. He does not want people to know God or to love him. This is why the devil tempts Jesus. He wants to keep Jesus from showing people what God is like. So the devil tells Jesus to worship *him*, not God.

The story tells us that this temptation was very serious and hard to resist. But Jesus doesn't listen. He understands that it is very important that people get to know God better. Nothing will stop Jesus from doing what he has to do.

When he resists this temptation, Jesus is not thinking of himself. More important to Jesus than anything is his mission—serving God and telling people what God is really like.

Sometimes people with a lot of power use that power only for themselves. Sometimes congressmen or presidents or people who run large companies don't think of the people who work for them, but only of what they can get for themselves. They want to be famous and rich and powerful, no matter what happens to the people they are supposed to be taking care of.

Jesus was the Son of God, the King. He was more powerful than anyone. He could tell people exactly what God wanted and what God was like. He could do all sorts of miracles. No other king could do that. Jesus could have used his power to become rich and famous, to have a large kingdom with a beautiful palace, and everything else kings had in those days. But Jesus wanted nothing to do with any of that. His only thought was to serve God. The reason why any of us know God is because Jesus wouldn't listen to the tempter, and refused to use his power for himself.

**Lesson 30**

Matthew 13:53–58
# Jesus' Hometown
# Does Not Accept Him

*What the Parent Should Know: Opposition to Jesus did not come just from the Roman government or Jewish leadership. It came from those who knew him best. They saw the boy grow up as a carpenter's son. They knew his family. And here he is, walking into the synagogue and teaching. This is not something the working class does—only the educated, those who have studied with the rabbis.*

*Still, what Jesus taught amazed the people, and they couldn't get their heads around it. "How can someone like us teach this way?"*

*It is ironic that the Jewish leadership rejected Jesus because he wasn't one of them, whereas Jesus' town folk rejected him because he was. As Jesus says in Matthew 8:20, "Foxes have holes and birds of the air have nests, but the Son of Man has no place to rest his head."*

*Children should learn that Jesus lived a life of rejection. Even his closest disciples turned from him at the end. Often, Jesus was unpopular and unwelcome.*

*Our own lives, children's included, are sometimes marked by similar times of isolation in our Christian journeys. During those times it is helpful for us to know that we are following in the master's footsteps.*

*Begin by reading aloud:*

> When Jesus had finished these parables, he moved on from there.
>
> Coming to his hometown, he began teaching the people in their synagogue, and they were amazed. "Where did this man get this wisdom and these miraculous powers?" they asked. "Isn't this the carpenter's son? Isn't his mother's name Mary, and aren't his brothers James, Joseph, Simon and Judas? Aren't all his sisters with us? Where then did this man get all these things?" And they took offense at him.
>
> But Jesus said to them, "Only in his hometown and in his own house is a prophet without honor."
>
> And he did not do many miracles there because of their lack of faith.

Jesus was not always welcomed by others. He was not always popular. He was famous, and people knew who he was. But many times, he was not accepted or even liked. Sometimes it seemed like everyone was against him, even the people who knew him best.

Jesus grew up in the town of Nazareth. People knew him. They had watched him grow up. They knew his mother, Mary, and his father, Joseph. They knew his brothers and sisters.

As a grown man, Jesus came back to his hometown and began teaching in the synagogue. Remember, a synagogue is where the Jews of Jesus' day went to study and learn about God. (Synagogues still exist today all over the world.)

But this surprised the people of his hometown. They knew Jesus as Joseph's son, the son of a carpenter. In those days, carpenters did not go to school to learn how to teach the Bible, and they certainly did not teach in a synagogue. Teaching was something that only rabbis did. They were the only teachers who were trained in school to read the Bible and explain it. The people of Nazareth felt that Jesus had no business doing what he did. It bothered them that Jesus was teaching them about God, and so they did not want to listen.

In this story, we see that although Jesus came to tell people about God, people were not always open to listening to him. Everywhere Jesus went, there were people against him. Sometimes the Roman government was against him. Sometimes the leaders of the synagogues fought with him. And here even the people of his hometown turned against him.

Jesus lived a life of rejection. He was not always liked. In fact, there were some people who hated him. This can happen to us, too. Following Jesus sometimes means that others will not like us, and we might feel very alone. Jesus knows exactly how that feels.

## Lesson 31

## Matthew 12:38–42

## Greater than Jonah and Solomon

*What the Parent Should Know: Occasionally, Jesus' opponents wanted to see some proof that he was the messiah, some miraculous sign. Jesus was not in the habit of becoming a dog-and-pony show, and he took these moments as an opportunity to call out his opponents for their inability to recognize him (note he calls them a "wicked and adulterous generation" for asking for a sign, v. 39).*

The "sign" he gives them is really no sign at all. It is a Bible lesson. First, he appeals to the story of Jonah as an illustration of what he will endure later. The well-known story of Jonah's three days and nights in the belly of the fish parallels Jesus' time in the tomb before his resurrection.

Jonah brought the message of repentance to the Gentile Ninevites, and even these Gentiles were able to recognize the message and repent. But now, someone greater than Jonah is here, and the leaders of God's own people, the Jews, don't get it. This "sign" is a slap in the face to the Jewish leaders, saying that the Gentiles have more sense than they do.

The reference to Solomon and the Queen of the South has the same purpose (see 1 Kings 10:1–13). Known as the Queen of Sheba in the Old Testament story (southern Arabia, modern-day Yemen), she, too is a Gentile like the Ninevites. And like the Ninevites, she, too, recognizes the wisdom of the Israelite King, Solomon. The Pharisees and teachers of the law, however, who of all people should know better, cannot see what is right in front of them.

Jesus is announcing to his opponents that he is the supreme prophet and king, and he will not accommodate their distrustful challenge and give his credentials. In fact, he had already performed miracles that didn't convince them, and that they actually tried to turn against him (see Matthew 12:22–24). Here he is saying, "Enough."

The first sign, therefore, is not something he would do now in their midst. Nor is it something that has already happened. It is something that has yet to happen: his resurrection. Jesus seems to be saying, "You won't believe what I have done so far, so your next sign is something you will have to wait for. But the sign is like what happened to Jonah."

This doesn't satisfy them, but then again, Jesus was not interested in doing that. He was more interested in denouncing them for their lack of recognition.

Begin by reading aloud:

Then some of the Pharisees and teachers of the law said to him, "Teacher, we want to see a miraculous sign from you."

He answered, "A wicked and adulterous generation asks for a miraculous sign! But none will be given it except the sign of the prophet Jonah. For as Jonah was three days and three nights in the belly of a huge fish, so the Son of Man will be three days and three nights in the heart of the earth. The men of Nineveh will stand up at the judgment with this generation and condemn it; for they repented at the preaching of Jonah, and now one greater than Jonah is here. The Queen of the South will rise at the judgment with this generation and condemn it; for she came from the ends of the earth to listen to Solomon's wisdom, and now one greater than Solomon is here."

In this passage, Jesus talks about two Old Testament stories. First he mentions the story of the prophet Jonah. God commanded Jonah to tell the people of Nineveh about him, but Jonah did not want to. The people of Nineveh were Israel's enemies, and Jonah really wanted God to punish them, not help them. So Jonah tried to run away from God by taking a boat trip to a place called Tarshish. On the way, God sent a storm, and the crew was frightened. Jonah told them that God was angry with him, not them, and if they threw him overboard, the storm would stop. So they did—and Jonah was swallowed by a big fish. Three days later the fish spit Jonah back onto the land.

The other story Jesus talks about is the Queen of the South. ("South" means the southern part of Arabia.) She was a queen from a very important country, but she had heard of King Solomon's great wisdom. She made the long trip from Arabia to Israel to see for herself.

Why does Jesus talk about these Old Testament stories? Because Israel's leaders did not believe that Jesus was sent by God and they wanted him to prove it. They wanted a sign.

It's funny that the people in Jesus' day who were the most against him were the people who really should have known better. These were the religious leaders, those who were teachers of the Bible. They were the ones responsible for teaching the people about God. And here was Jesus, God's Son, and they couldn't even recognize him.

Jesus had been doing all sorts of miracles, but these leaders still didn't believe him. "Show us another miracle," they said. But Jesus wouldn't do it. "You should know by now who I am," Jesus said.

He does not give them a sign, but he does tell them about Jonah and the Queen of the South. Jonah was in the belly of the fish for three days. This is like Jesus, who would be raised from the dead three days after he was crucified. Jesus just says, "You don't believe me now, so you'll have to wait for me to rise from the dead."

The same thing happens with the Queen of the South. Jesus is still not giving his enemies a sign. He is saying, "This queen who is not even an Israelite knew how great Solomon was. But I am greater even than Solomon, and you Israelite leaders don't get it."

Put yourself in Jesus' place to understand how he felt. Imagine that you really want to show your family that you want to help around the house. So day after day, you do a lot of chores. You keep your room clean and pick up toys around the house. You put your dirty clothes in the laundry basket. Maybe you walk the dog, take out the garbage, or help clean up the yard.

You do this not just for a day or two, but day after day for a whole month. You do all this because you really want to be kind and help the family.

But what if no one notices? In fact, what if your brother or sister comes up to you and says, "Hey, we want to know whether you really want to help out in the house. How about doing some work around here for a change?" You might have the same reaction Jesus had. "Forget it. Haven't you been paying attention? I'm not going to prove myself to you!"

This is the kind of thing that happened to Jesus all through the Gospel stories. People were listening to him talk, but they still kept saying, "Prove yourself to us." If they had truly been paying attention, they would have known that Jesus was speaking for God.

## Lesson 32

John 7:25–31

# Jesus' Time Had Not Yet Come

*What the Parent Should Know: This passage is found in a section of John's Gospel that deals with numerous rejections of, and oppositions to, Jesus. Jesus' authority is regularly questioned. The confrontation recorded in this passage is part of a larger passage that begins in v. 14 and ends at v. 44, although we can treat the smaller portion here because it contains a couple of distinct topics.*

*First, we see the recurring question of Jesus' identity. In the previous passage, Jesus claims the authority to heal on the Sabbath (vv. 23–24). This brings the crowd to ask how it is that Jesus can keep talking like this, knowing that there was a plot to kill him. "Why don't they just get on with it?" they ask.*

*This raises an idea in the minds of some of the crowd: maybe the authorities have concluded that Jesus is in fact the messiah! That's why they don't kill him. But even if the authorities have accepted Jesus, these members of the crowd will not, because (as they say) Jesus' identity is known, whereas no one will know where the messiah comes from. (There was apparently* disagreement among the Jews of the time about whether the Old Testament revealed the origin of the messiah.)

But Jesus does not enter the debate about the earthly origins of the messiah. He shifts the focus, claiming that his true origin is from God. His opponents here felt that if they could peg him as a Nazarene, they could disqualify his messianic claims; Jesus simply responds that he is indeed from Nazareth ("you know me"), but more importantly, he is sent by the Father ("You do not know him," v. 28).

If Jesus' goal is to win friends, this is not the way to go about it. This claim to be intimate with God the Father, along with the suggestion that his opponents do not know God because they do not recognize the Son, sends the people into a frenzy again. Some put their faith in him, but by and large the crowd wants him dead. But Jesus' time for this has not come, and so they are not able to carry out their plan.

A central point of John's Gospel can be grasped here. Even though Jesus suffered hostile opposition, his end was not the result of a failed plan. It was, so to speak, a "planned failure." His purpose was to die at the right time: God's time.

Begin by reading aloud:

> At that point some of the people of Jerusalem began to ask, "Isn't this the man they are trying to kill? Here he is, speaking publicly, and they are not saying a word to him. Have the authorities really concluded that he is the Christ? But we know where this man is from; when the Christ comes, no one will know where he is from."
>
> Then Jesus, still teaching in the temple courts, cried out, "Yes, you know me, and you know where I am from. I am not here on my own, but he who sent me is true. You do not know him, but I know him because I am from him and he sent me."
>
> At this they tried to seize him, but no one laid a hand on him, because his time had not yet come. Still, many in the crowd put their faith in him. They said, "When the Christ comes, will he do more miraculous signs than this man?"

In this story, Jesus has been teaching at a feast in the temple. (A feast is a religious holiday.) This was in Jerusalem, the biggest and most important city in Judea. There were a lot of people there—a huge crowd—and many of them did not at all like what Jesus had to say. He was claiming to be sent by God. He said that, since God sent him, he knew God better than anyone. He also told the crowd that they were not able to understand the things he was telling them.

This was not the first time Jesus talked like this. By now, the people knew that the religious leaders wanted to kill him for saying such things! They were surprised that Jesus had enough nerve to show up at this holiday, in such a huge crowd, talking the way he did.

So here is Jesus, in Jerusalem, with a big feast going on, and everyone is after him.

Can you imagine being somewhere in public—a big movie theater, or a stadium, or a shopping mall—and realizing that everyone there is so angry with you that they want to hurt you? The only people on your side are a few of your friends. Of course, that won't happen to you. But it did happen to Jesus.

But even the large crowd could not hurt him. Jesus kept right on teaching, even though people were growing angrier and angrier. Some of the people tried to grab Jesus to make him stop talking. But they were not able to do anything to him. Why? Because it wasn't yet the right time for Jesus to die. That time had been planned by God and would come later. Because God's plan was not yet complete, the crowd was powerless against Jesus.

# Unit 8

# The End of Jesus' Life

For the Parent: The four Gospels all have different emphases and nuances, but one area where there is considerable overlap is the account of the Passion Week, the last week of Jesus' life.

Although the focus of the Passion Week accounts is certainly on Jesus' death and resurrection, there are numerous other events of the week that contribute to the overall portrait of Jesus that is being painted: his entry to Jerusalem, which caused a stir for all sorts of reasons; Jesus' move to confront the religious leaders rather than align with them; the circumstances surrounding his trial; the true tragedy of his death and triumph of his resurrection. The events of this week show the final purpose of Jesus' life and are a bridge to the remaining books of the New Testament.

The purpose of this unit is not to cover the entire story of Jesus' death and resurrection, but rather to begin to study some parts of it in depth. The later years of this curriculum will return to this story again and again to complete the student's understanding.

The assumption is that the student will have already heard the full story in other contexts. However, if you wish to add to this unit, you may read selections from Matthew 27–28, Mark 15–16, Luke 23–24, or John 19–20.

# Matthew 21:1–11
# Jesus Rides into Jerusalem as a King

*What the Parent Should Know: When Jesus rode into Jerusalem on a donkey at the beginning of the Easter week, his entrance was not primarily a sign of humility. Rather, he was declaring his kingship, as indicated by the quotation from Zechariah 9:9 ("see, your king comes to you"). This is why he was cheered by the inhabitants of Jerusalem. The messianic hope of Jesus' day was for someone to deliver the Jews from Roman bondage, and so reestablish Jewish independence in the homeland. The messiah would also lead the people in obedience to God, which the Jews thought of as obedience to the Law. The messiah, in other words, would ride into Jerusalem with a Torah in one hand and a sword in the other.*

*Anyone present at this event would have recognized Jesus' self-declaration of kingship. But as we see throughout Passion Week, Jesus' notion of what it meant to be king had little to do with a military conquest. Jesus deliberately failed to meet the expectations of the Palm Sunday crowd throughout the week. He did not come to deliver Israel, but to pass judgment on Israel.*

*For example, Jesus overturns the tables in the temple (Matthew 21:12–13). On one level, he is angry that the temple has taken on almost a carnival atmosphere, but there is more to it. Money changers were not in and of themselves a negative thing. They were important for the functioning of the temple, for this allowed pilgrims to exchange foreign currency and buy the doves for the sacrifice rather than having to carry their own animals on the journey. By cleansing the temple, Jesus was not just condemning its abuse. He was also saying, "I am here, and now you won't be needing this any longer."*

*Jesus came as a king, but a very different one than was expected. The kingdom of God is not to be equated with Jewish independence or faithfulness to Torah. Jesus is about to do something new.*

*Begin by reading aloud:*

> As they approached Jerusalem and came to Bethphage on the Mount of Olives, Jesus sent two disciples, saying to them, "Go to the village ahead of you, and at once you will find a donkey tied there, with her colt by her. Untie them and bring them to me. If anyone says anything

to you, tell him that the Lord needs them, and he will send them right away."

This took place to fulfill what was spoken through the prophet: "Say to the Daughter of Zion, 'See, your king comes to you, gentle and riding on a donkey, on a colt, the foal of a donkey.'"

The disciples went and did as Jesus had instructed them. They brought the donkey and the colt, placed their cloaks on them, and Jesus sat on them. A very large crowd spread their cloaks on the road, while others cut branches from the trees and spread them on the road. The crowds that went ahead of him and those that followed shouted, "Hosanna to the Son of David!" "Blessed is he who comes in the name of the Lord!"

"Hosanna in the highest!"

When Jesus entered Jerusalem, the whole city was stirred and asked, "Who is this?"

The crowds answered, "This is Jesus, the prophet from Nazareth in Galilee."

One week before Easter we celebrate Palm Sunday. This is the day that Jesus rode into Jerusalem on a donkey. There was a very large crowd there, and they were cheering loudly.

Jerusalem was the capital of Israel, sort of like Washington, D.C., is the capital of the United States. The people of Jerusalem were worried and unhappy, though. The Romans had taken over Jerusalem many years earlier. The people of Jerusalem did not like being ruled by the Romans. They wanted their own king who would come and take the country back from the Romans and give it to the Jews.

Riding on a donkey is what this king was supposed to do. The donkey was a little bit like the special airplane that the president of the United States uses when he flies from city to city. The president's plane is called Air Force One. When Air Force One lands in the airport, everyone *knows* who is in it!

When Jesus rode into Jerusalem on a donkey, everyone knew that their king was here.

So they cheered loudly when Jesus rode by. The crowd was shouting "Hosanna." That is a word that means "save." That is what they were expecting from Jesus, to save them. If Jesus was their king, they wanted his help.

Jesus was a king, but not the kind of king the people expected. Jesus did not enter Jerusalem as a warrior or conqueror. He did not come to start a war against the Romans. This is what the people wanted, but Jesus was not going to give it to them. Jesus came to Jerusalem for a much bigger reason. He came to save the people from their sins.

But the people did not understand this. They were cheering, but for the wrong reasons. By the end of the week, Jesus would be all alone.

---

## Lesson 34

## Matthew 21:18–22

## A Fig Tree

*What the Parent Should Know: Immediately after Jesus cleansed the temple, he performed what might seem at first glance like a petty act: he withered a fig tree that was not bearing fruit. What is the meaning of this gesture?*

*Much of what happens between Matthew 21 and 25 can be summed up in 21:43: "the kingdom of God will be taken away from you and given to a people who will produce its fruit." Fig trees at this time of year were supposed to be bearing fruit. At the "season" of his appearance in Jerusalem, the proper response of the children of Israel as a whole would be to "bear fruit" in keeping with the kingdom— which would begin with acknowledging Jesus as the messiah.*

*Jesus had many followers among the children of Israel, particularly among the poor, the oppressed, and other outsiders who were looked down upon by many in the ruling class. The turn to Jesus did not happen as completely as his presence among them deserved. In this sense, Jesus says that the fig tree is barren. By withering the fig tree, Jesus pronounces judgment on those who refuse to accept him. They have failed to bear fruit, by failing to model both faith in Jesus and what a godly people should look like. Hence, the kingdom will be given to others, to those who will bear fruit. The citizens of the kingdom will include those who were considered on the outside: tax collectors, prostitutes, and even Gentiles.*

*Israel's hope was for its messiah to come and set up his rule in Jerusalem. He was to rule over the Israelites as a free people and to maintain their distinct identity as THE people of God, true members of God's kingdom, keepers of the Law. But Jesus is taking that right away from them and giving it to others—the very people from whom law-abiding Jews wanted to distance themselves: sinners and Gentiles. This message was deeply offensive to the Jewish leadership, and directly contributed to Jesus' death sentence later that week.*

*The disciples' reaction to the fig tree is understandable: "How can this happen so quickly?" The quickness with which the fig tree withered symbolizes the swiftness with which judgment against Israel was being carried out—something already begun in the temple cleansing in the previous section.*

*Verses 21–22 do not teach that followers of Jesus will be able to do anything if they believe and pray hard enough. Rather, the disciples, too, will be active participants in establishing this kingdom and will do amazing things in the process.*

*This episode may seem like an arbitrary trick for children, almost a temper tantrum. But it is a concrete symbol of Jesus ushering in a new kind of kingdom that will include all who believe, not just Israel.*

*Begin by reading aloud:*

> Early in the morning, as he was on his way back to the city, he was hungry.
>
> Seeing a fig tree by the road, he went up to it but found nothing on it except leaves. Then he said to it, "May you never bear fruit again!" Immediately the tree withered.
>
> When the disciples saw this, they were amazed. "How did the fig tree wither so quickly?" they asked.
>
> Jesus replied, "I tell you the truth, if you have faith and do not doubt, not only can you do what was done to the fig tree, but also you can say to this mountain, 'Go, throw yourself into the sea,' and it will be done. If you believe, you will receive whatever you ask for in prayer."

Fig trees were everywhere in Jesus' day. Figs are a kind of fruit that is sweet and tasty. Anyone who got hungry could just go to a fig tree and pick a fig or two and eat.

But this fig tree did not have any figs on it, even though it was springtime, when trees were supposed to be blooming and bearing fruit. When Jesus saw that there were no figs on this tree, he said, "No more figs for you—ever," and the tree withered (it became dry and shriveled).

That probably sounds a bit weird, like Jesus was having a temper tantrum because he was hungry. But Jesus wasn't mad at the fig tree. He could have walked to another tree very near by and had some figs. Jesus was not having a temper tantrum, like we sometimes have when we want a snack *right now* but can't have one. Jesus withered the tree because he wanted to teach his disciples a lesson, not about fig trees but about believing in God.

When Jesus rode into Jerusalem a couple of days earlier, the crowd wanted him to be their king. But not everyone wanted to listen to Jesus and what he had to tell them about God. They wanted Jesus to be the kind of king they wanted. They wanted a king who would have soldiers and go to war against the Romans. But Jesus said that his kingdom was not about wars. It was about loving God and knowing God.

This is why Jesus withered the fig tree in front of his disciples. He was teaching them that he wanted nothing to do with those people who were searching for the wrong kind of king. He told the fig tree, "I am finished with you." And he was saying to those people who wanted the wrong kind of king, "I am done with you—no more."

## Lesson 35

## Matthew 21:23–27
## Jesus Outsmarts the Religious Leaders

*What the Parent Needs to Know: Following upon the heels of the temple cleansing and withering of the fig tree, Jesus goes back to the temple to teach. This is quite a bold move, since his last appearance in the temple (when he turned over the tables of the money changers) would not have won him many friends among temple leaders.*

*This is a wonderful example of Jesus' ability to go toe-to-toe with the religious leaders and outwit them. When the leaders asked, "By what authority are you doing these things?" it was not a polite question. "These things" likely refers to the temple cleansing and healing earlier that week (21:12–17), as well as Jesus' audacity at coming back to teach. The leaders were saying, in effect, "Who do you think you are, marching in here, on our turf, in our temple, disrupting things and now teaching?" Not only was Jesus an established troublemaker, but he was not of the elite teaching class.*

*So in response, Jesus poses a question concerning the baptism of John, knowing that any answer they give would be condemning. Their refusal to answer exposes the leaders for the corrupt and dishonest lot they are.*

*By answering their question with another question, Jesus answers them indirectly. He shows that they themselves, by their duplicity, do not have true authority to lead God's people. (Also, his response exhibits his own cleverness in contrast to the religious leaders who so easily fall into his trap.)*

*It is good for children to see that their Savior has some teeth. Jesus was bold and confrontational when he needed to be. His purpose here, as in much of Passion Week, was to bring judgment to Israel—especially to the leaders who should have known better. He was brushing them aside to make room for a new version of the people of God, one that included sinners and Gentiles.*

*In other words, Jesus' actions here are not a model of behavior for Christians today to become belligerent when they have theological differences with other Christians.*

*Begin by reading aloud:*

> Jesus entered the temple courts, and, while he was teaching, the chief priests and the elders of the people came to him. "By what authority are you doing these things?" they asked. "And who gave you this authority?"
>
> Jesus replied, "I will also ask you one question. If you answer me, I will tell you by what authority I am doing these things. John's baptism—where did it come from? Was it from heaven, or from men?"
>
> They discussed it among themselves and said, "If we say, 'From heaven,' he will ask, 'Then why didn't you believe him?' But if we say, 'From men'—we are afraid of the people, for they all hold that John was a prophet."
>
> So they answered Jesus, "We don't know."
>
> Then he said, "Neither will I tell you by what authority I am doing these things."

Has anyone ever tried to push you around, to bully you? In this story, the religious leaders—the "priests and elders"—were trying to bully Jesus.

By now they were very irritated with Jesus. He had been going around telling people what God was really like. Often, Jesus told the people that what they were learning about God from the religious leaders was just plain wrong.

This didn't make the religious leaders happy!

When Jesus came to the temple to teach, the leaders couldn't believe it. Jesus had a lot of nerve showing up in the temple after all he had been saying about the leaders! So they ganged up on Jesus and tried to get rid of him. "Who do think you are, Jesus? What gives you the right to say the things you have been saying?" That is what they meant when they asked Jesus "By what authority are you doing these things?"

The religious leaders thought Jesus was like a child who walks into a classroom full of students and teachers and begins telling everyone what to do. They felt Jesus had no business coming to the temple, telling them what to do. So they challenged him with a question: "What gives you the right to say what you have been saying and then come here?"

So Jesus asked them a question about John the Baptist. John the Baptist was related to Jesus—his mother and Jesus' mother were cousins. Before Jesus began to preach and do miracles, John the Baptist began calling people to repent, or to turn away from their sins. He did this to get them ready to hear Jesus' words. Then he baptized those who repented—he washed them in the Jordan River to show that they had been washed clean of their past sins.

The people of Jesus' day thought very highly of John the Baptist. He baptized people so they could begin a new relationship with God. He was doing God's work.

So instead of answering the question about his authority, Jesus asks the leaders, "Tell me, where did John get the authority to baptize, from heaven or from men?" (That means "from God or from a person.") "If you can answer that question, I will answer your question."

Jesus was not afraid to answer them. Not at all. He could have said, "My authority comes from God. He sent me." But Jesus wanted to outwit them. He wanted to show everyone there that the religious leaders did not really know God.

The leaders did not know how to answer Jesus. They felt trapped. If they said "God gave him the authority," Jesus would have said, "OK, if that's what you think, why didn't you listen to him? John believed in me. Why don't you?"

If the religious leaders had answered that John got his authority from someone else, that would have gotten them in trouble, too. The people thought that John's authority came from God. They trusted and respected John the Baptist. If the religious leaders said "John wasn't sent by God," then the people would be very upset. They might even riot.

That is why the religious leaders said, "We don't know." No matter what answer they would give, they would be in some sort of trouble. They thought they were clever, but Jesus had made them look foolish. He knew that they were too proud to listen to him—and that they were leading others astray.

# Jesus' Crucifixion Is Near

*What the Parent Should Know:*
*There are two episodes told in this passage. First, Jesus connects his own impending death with the Passover (vv. 1–5), a feast that commemorated Israel's exodus from Egypt. The implication, which Paul draws out later, is that Jesus is the "Passover lamb" (I Corinthians 5:7). The chief priests and elders, however, want to avoid arresting Jesus during Passover. With a multitude of pilgrims in Jerusalem, not to mention the political tensions between Jews and Romans, the leaders have every right to be concerned about a riot of some sort. So they begin plotting to "arrest Jesus in some sly way and kill him" (v. 4).*

*The following scene takes place in Bethany, at the home of Simon the Leper, which suggests that Simon had been healed by Jesus. It was common to put some oil on guests' heads to freshen them up (so to speak). But the woman in this story used a very expensive oil. According to Mark 14:3 and John 12:3, the oil was nard, a more expensive oil than what was typically used for such purposes. Not only was the oil expensive, but she seems to have used a lot of it (again, a point made clearer in the other Gospels).*

*It was in one sense a "waste" of very expensive oil to pour it on a guest's head and have it running down his clothes and onto the floor. One can understand the disciples' reaction. But anointing with oil was also customary preparation for burial—and not just a bit on the head, but all over the body. The woman's act of utter devotion to Jesus was, unknown to her or to the disciples, a symbolic representation of Jesus' impending death.*

*Lastly, Jesus' comment about the poor always being with them does not indicate a callous indifference to their plight. Rather, he is saying that now is the time to focus on the events at hand. The disciples will have a continued obligation to those in need (as was the topic of his last parable, the sheep and goats; Matthew 25:31–46).*

*The inevitability of Jesus' crucifixion is now clear. Those who hold the power are plotting his death with intrigue and calculation. He has also been anointed for his burial before the fact, even though his closest followers still do not understand. Events leading to Jesus' crucifixion will continue to unfold quickly.*

*Begin by reading aloud:*

When Jesus had finished saying all these things, he said to his disciples, "As you know, the Passover is two days away—and the Son of Man will be handed over to be crucified."

Then the chief priests and the elders of the people assembled in the palace of the high priest, whose name was Caiaphas, and they plotted to arrest Jesus in some sly way and kill him. "But not during the Feast," they said, "or there may be a riot among the people."

While Jesus was in Bethany in the home of a man known as Simon the Leper, a woman came to him with an alabaster jar of very expensive perfume, which she poured on his head as he was reclining at the table.

When the disciples saw this, they were indignant. "Why this waste?" they asked. "This perfume could have been sold at a high price and the money given to the poor."

Aware of this, Jesus said to them, "Why are you bothering this woman? She has done a beautiful thing to me. The poor you will always have with you, but you will not always have me. When she poured this perfume on my body, she did it to prepare me for burial. I tell you the truth, wherever this Gospel is preached throughout the world, what she has done will also be told, in memory of her."

When you take a bath and wash your hair, you take a tiny little bit of shampoo and put it on your hair. Then you rub it in and rinse it out.

You don't take the whole bottle and just keep pouring. That would go all over the place and be a big waste. And what a mess it would be if your mother took a big bucket of shampoo and just dumped the whole thing all over you.

This story is about Jesus when he is very close to being crucified. He is having dinner at a friend's house, Simon. Simon used to be a leper, but Jesus healed him.

Back then, to get ready for dinner—to freshen up—people would put a little oil on their heads to smell nicer. (They didn't have nice shampoos or deodorants back then.) But this woman in the story went overboard. She took the whole jar of very expensive perfume and dumped the whole thing on Jesus.

She did that because she wanted to show Jesus how much she respected him. But the disciples thought it was not good to waste so much good oil just for a dinner. They complained that the oil could have been sold and the money given to the poor.

The disciples were not wrong to think this way, but there was something that they and the woman did not understand. Jesus knew that the leaders were getting ready to kill him later that week. Jesus knew he was going to be crucified. Oil was used not just to make people smell nice before dinner. It was also used to make a body smell better before it was buried. Bodies had to be buried pretty quickly back then because of the smell, and putting oil on the bodies helped a bit.

When Jesus told his disciples not to worry that so much oil was being wasted, it was his way of telling them that he was preparing to die later that week.

Supplemental Lessons

# The Rest of the Story

For the Parent: We did not want to end Year One without giving an overview of how the story ends: with Jesus' trial, death, and resurrection. These three episodes will be revisited in detail in more advanced levels of this curriculum, but younger students should also get a clear sense of where the story of Jesus is ultimately going.

Matthew, Mark, and Luke all have their distinct ways of telling the story of the crucifixion and resurrection. These supplemental lessons, however, are all taken from John's Gospel, which includes some stories that are not included in the other Gospels (e.g., the "doubting Thomas" episode and the appearance to Mary). By focusing on John in the supplemental lessons, the children can get to know John's Jesus a bit better.

**Lesson 1**

**John 18:33–40**

## The King Is on Trial

*What the Parent Should Know: Jesus was arrested at the beginning of chapter 18. After his arrest, he was brought first before Annas, the father-in-law of the high priest Caiaphas, and then to Caiaphas himself. During those inter-*

rogations, Peter, waiting outside, denied Jesus three times. (See John 18:1–27 for all of this.)

As we have seen throughout the Gospels, Jesus was quite capable of handling himself when challenged by authority figures, and the scene before Annas is no different (see vv. 19–24). Neither Annas nor Caiaphas knew what to do with Jesus, so they brought him to the Roman governor Pilate, who did not fare much better. He first tried getting out of the responsibility of making a decision about Jesus by telling the crowd that they should take care of this in-house matter on their own (vv. 28–32). The crowd would have none of that, however. They wanted blood, and so Pilate proceeded with his interrogation—and this is where our passage begins.

Pilate's concern boils down to one thing: he wants to know if Jesus poses any sort of credible political threat to him. Is Jesus just another in a line of rebels who wants to move Pilate aside and restore Jewish rule over Judea? This is the meaning of the question in v. 33 "Are you the king of the Jews?"

The simple answer to this question would have been for Jesus to say, "No, of course not. I've been telling people left and right that I am not interested in your throne. I am falsely accused by jealous Jewish leaders of wanting to rebel against you. They are using you to get to me. You can let me go." But instead, Jesus uses this moment to make a point about who he is and what his mission is.

First, he probes Pilate a bit to see whether he really understands what "king of the Jews" means (v. 34). But this line of questioning annoys Pilate—after all, Jesus is on trial here, not him. His response is, "Listen, I'm not a Jew. Your people handed you over to me and now I've got to try to find a way through this mess. So tell me, what have you done to get them to hand you over to me?" (v. 35).

Jesus' famous answer in v. 36 is wholly truthful, consistent with what he has been saying throughout his ministry, and puts Pilate's mind at ease: "My kingdom is not of this world." Pilate seems relieved, but that is not at all Jesus' intention. The fact that Jesus' kingdom is not of this world should actually be more of a threat to Pilate—he is accountable to Jesus, THE king (v. 37). In this kingdom, Pilate himself is a subject, not a master.

But Pilate does not understand Jesus' point, and he is not impressed. He blows Jesus off with a flippant response, "What is truth?" (v. 38), which is the functional equivalent of "Yeah, yeah. Whatever." Still, although Pilate thinks Jesus is a fool, Jesus has done nothing to warrant a death sentence. Pilate knows he needs to let the prisoner go. But Pilate truly is a king of "this world": he is enough of a politician to know that he can't just let Jesus walk without incurring the anger of a large crowd of people. He appeals to the custom of releasing one

*Jewish prisoner at Passover—he was offering a political olive branch (v. 39). He would like to make Jesus that one prisoner, but the crowd will not have it. They want Barabbas released instead—a man who poses an actual political threat, and who had been arrested for his part in a previous rebellion (v. 40).*

*Begin the lesson by reading aloud:*

> Pilate then went back inside the palace, summoned Jesus and asked him, "Are you the king of the Jews?"
>
> "Is that your own idea," Jesus asked, "or did others talk to you about me?"
>
> "Am I a Jew?" Pilate replied. "It was your people and your chief priests who handed you over to me. What is it you have done?"
>
> Jesus said, "My kingdom is not of this world. If it were, my servants would fight to prevent my arrest by the Jews. But now my kingdom is from another place."
>
> "You are a king, then!" said Pilate.
>
> Jesus answered, "You are right in saying I am a king. In fact, for this reason I was born, and for this I came into the world, to testify to the truth. Everyone on the side of truth listens to me."
>
> "What is truth?" Pilate asked. With this he went out again to the Jews and said, "I find no basis for a charge against him. But it is your custom for me to release to you one prisoner at the time of the Passover. Do you want me to release 'the king of the Jews'?"
>
> They shouted back, "No, not him! Give us Barabbas!" Now Barabbas had taken part in a rebellion.

By the end of his life, Jesus had made a lot of people angry with him. Some of his enemies wanted him to be put to death, so they brought him before two religious leaders, Annas and his son-in-law Caiaphas. Caiaphas was the high priest at the time, and Annas had been high priest before him. High priests were the main leaders of the Jews. The Romans had taken over Judea and the Jewish government—so the Romans were in charge of picking the high priests, and the high priests had to obey Roman laws and do what the Romans told them to do.

Annas and Caiaphas were the most powerful of the Jewish leaders. They were tired of Jesus challenging the authority of the Jewish leaders and telling the people not to listen to them. They wanted to put him to death, but the law would not allow them to give someone a death sentence. So they sent him to Pilate. Pilate was the Roman governor over the Jews, and he had the authority to put someone to death.

But Pilate didn't want anything to do with Jesus, either. Why? Because he could see that Jesus had not done anything wrong. That is why he asked Jesus whether he was "king of the Jews." Pilate was trying to find out whether Jesus wanted to rebel against him and take over his job.

In answer, Jesus told Pilate that he *was* a king, but that his kingdom was not in the land of Judea. Instead, Jesus said, "My kingdom is not of this world." That is Jesus' way of saying that he was sent by God to be a different kind of king. He is not a king with a palace, or guards, or soldiers. He is not a rebel who wants to take over the government. Jesus is the kind of king who tells people the truth about God.

Pilate understood that Jesus was not going to rebel against him and the Roman government. So he wanted to let him go, but the crowd outside wanted nothing to do with that idea. They did not like what Jesus had to say about God, and they wanted Pilate to put him to death.

Pilate wanted to let Jesus go, and he had an idea. It was a custom for Pilate to let one prisoner go each year. A man named Barabbas was in prison because he was a real rebel, so Pilate gave the people a choice: "Do you want me to let Jesus go or Barabbas?" Pilate thought the people would pick Jesus, since Barabbas really was a criminal. But the crowd was all worked up against Jesus. They said, "No, not him. Give us Barabbas." Jesus' trial before Pilate was over. Now he would be crucified.

**Lesson 2**

**John 19:17–27**

# The Crucifixion

*What the Parent Should Know: Crucifixion was a horrible and shameful means of execution. This was the way common criminals, slaves, and revolutionaries died, and the Romans made sure the punishment got their message across: disruption of Roman law and order will not be tolerated.*

*Our image of crucifixion is too easily influenced by much of the history of Christian art and crucifixes we wear. But in reality crucifixion was disgusting. Victims were sometimes hung in cruel and unusual positions, naked, and in indescribable pain. It could take days for victims to die this way, all the while struggling to breathe by forcing themselves more upright*

Supplemental Lesson 2: The Crucifixion

against the weight of their own bodies—an act that caused intense pain in the arms and legs.

Jesus was crucified in the place known by its Aramaic name Golgotha, meaning skull. The better-known name "Calvary" is the Latin word known to the church through the Latin translation of the Bible, the Vulgate. Latin was the language of the Romans, but Greek and Aramaic (a sister language to Hebrew) were also in use. The popularity of all three languages can be seen in the sign that Pilate fastened to the cross, "Jesus of Nazareth, King of the Jews." (The well-known acronym INRI reflects the Latin: the Latin words for "Jesus" and "Jew" begin with an I, and the Latin word for king is rex.) The Jews requested that the wording be changed, but Pilate refused. This was not an act of faith on his part; probably it was his way of getting back at his Jewish subjects for insisting that Jesus be crucified.

The sign may also be mocking Jesus as well as warning other trouble-makers. Nazareth was a backwater burb (see John 1:46). By calling Jesus "The King of the Jews" Pilate was saying, "This is what happens to hillbillies who make trouble."

Jesus was stripped of all his clothes, which were divided among the soldiers. It seems that the even division of the clothing left the undergarment as the lone remaining piece. (The undergarment was likely more of a robe than what we think of as undergarments.) Because it was of one piece, the soldiers decided to cast lots for it rather than cut it up evenly among them. John ties this to Psalm 22, thus indicating another way in which the events of Jesus' life are connected to the Old Testament.

Jesus was likely surrounded by numerous people, some of whom are mentioned in v. 25. Jesus charged Mary to look on "the disciple whom he loved" (John) as her son, and for John to look on Mary as his mother. Among other things, this emphasizes the special bond between Jesus and John (see also 13:23; 20:2; 21:7, 20). It may also indicate that Jesus' own siblings were not in the position to take responsibility for Mary, perhaps because they did not acknowledge who Jesus was (see 7:5).

John's portrayal of the crucifixion has some overlap with the other Gospels, but the version is largely unique to him. There are two big themes here. First, John wants us to know that Jesus' crucifixion is not an afterthought; it is part of God's larger plan, which his appeal to Psalm 22 shows. John also shows that, despite what happened to Jesus, he is still king. Pilate's sign inadvertently declares that, even on the cross, Jesus is king. But he is not "King of the Jews" in the way Pilate meant to mock him. Jesus was not the earthly king, but the messiah whose kingdom is not of this world—a point Jesus made to Pilate earlier (18:36).

*Begin the lesson by reading aloud:*

Today's story tells us what happened after Jesus left his trial in front of Pilate. You will need to know that people in Jesus' day spoke three different languages—Aramaic, Latin, and Greek. If you wanted everyone to be able to read a sign, you would write it in all three languages.

Now listen to the story:

> The soldiers took charge of Jesus. Carrying his own cross, he went out to the place of the Skull (which in Aramaic is called Golgotha). Here they crucified him, and with him two others—one on each side and Jesus in the middle. Pilate had a notice prepared and fastened to the cross. It read: JESUS OF NAZARETH, THE KING OF THE JEWS.
>
> Many of the Jews read this sign, for the place where Jesus was crucified was near the city, and the sign was written in Aramaic, Latin and Greek. The chief priests of the Jews protested to Pilate, "Do not write 'The King of the Jews,' but that this man claimed to be king of the Jews."
>
> Pilate answered, "What I have written, I have written."
>
> When the soldiers crucified Jesus, they took his clothes, dividing them into four shares, one for each of them, with the undergarment remaining. This garment was seamless, woven in one piece from top to bottom.
>
> "Let's not tear it," they said to one another. "Let's decide by lot who will get it." This happened that the scripture might be fulfilled which said, "They divided my garments among them and cast lots for my clothing." So this is what the soldiers did.
>
> Near the cross of Jesus stood his mother, his mother's sister, Mary the wife of Clopas, and Mary Magdalene. When Jesus saw his mother there, and the disciple whom he loved standing nearby, he said to his mother, "Dear woman, here is your son," and to the disciple, "Here is your mother." From that time on, this disciple took her into his home.

Many Jews followed Jesus and believed him. But some powerful Jewish leaders wanted Jesus dead. Jesus had been telling the people that if they really wanted to know God, they should listen to him, not the religious leaders. This made those leaders very angry, and they wanted Pilate, the Roman governor, to put Jesus to death.

Pilate did not really want to put Jesus to death. He did not think Jesus had done anything wrong. Jesus wasn't trying to get rid of Pilate

**Supplemental Lesson 2: The Crucifixion**

and become the governor of Judea. He told Pilate that his kingdom was different. His kingdom was about telling people who God is and what it means to trust God.

But Pilate did not want to have more trouble from the leaders and from the big crowd outside his window. So Pilate agreed to crucify Jesus.

In most places in the world, if a criminal is executed for a crime, he probably did something really terrible, like killing innocent people. But there are other places in the world, even today, where people can be executed for things like stealing. Stealing is wrong, but you shouldn't be put to death for it. In some countries people are even put to death for changing their religion or disagreeing with the government. In Jesus' day, people could be put to death by the Roman government for all sorts of reasons. Roman rulers could put people to death pretty much whenever they felt like it.

If you live in a town, your town has a mayor—a leader who is in charge of running the town, just like Pilate was in charge of running Jerusalem. Imagine if the mayor just showed up at your front door, with police cars and sirens, and arrested your mother or father because some people down the street didn't like them very much. If you saw that happening, you would probably be frightened, helpless—powerless to do anything.

But Jesus was not powerless or helpless. Jesus was innocent, but the crucifixion was not an accident. God meant for this to happen to save the people from their sins, and Jesus carried out what God wanted. This is what John is talking about when he says, "This happened that the scripture might be fulfilled." He is thinking of Psalm 22, an Old Testament poem written hundreds and hundreds of years before Jesus lived. This poem talks about the crucifixion! John wants us to understand that the crucifixion was in God's mind long ago.

So, Jesus was crucified, and he died. He was buried in a tomb. And on the third day he rose from the dead.

John 20:1–9

# Jesus Is Alive Again

*What the Parent Should Know: John reports that Mary Magdalene was the first to come to the tomb. ("Magdalene" likely means that she came from Magdala, a town along the Sea of Galilee.) Although John's Gospel does not mention it, Mary was apparently coming back at the first opportunity after the Sabbath day ended to complete the burial preparation that had to be cut short on Friday (see John 19:42 and Mark 16:1). She came alone and saw that the stone had been removed, and so ran back to tell Peter and John ("the other disciple, the one Jesus loved," v. 2). Mary clearly had no thought of resurrection, for she told the disciples that Jesus' body had been "taken" and "we don't know where they have put him" (v. 2).*

*Peter and John heard the news and ran for the tomb. John got there first, and Peter followed behind. Both saw the strips of linen on the ground, and Peter actually ventured in. The linen strips pertain to Jewish burial practices (19:40), where strips of linen were wrapped around the body that had been prepared with spices. Inside the tomb Peter saw the burial cloth "folded up" and placed apart from the linen (v. 7; the Greek word may simply mean "rolled up," but the basic idea is the same). This seems like an unusual detail to mention, but the care with which the cloth had been left, not to mention the very fact that expensive linen was left behind, makes the case that neither grave robbers nor the disciples themselves were responsible for removing the body—either would have simply taken the body rather than taking the time to unwrap Jesus and then tidy up a bit.*

*After Peter viewed the scene, John came in and believed. John believed because he saw the empty tomb. Later, Thomas will insist on "seeing" before he believes (20:25), which seems reasonable, since that is what happens at the tomb with John. But Jesus will tell Thomas that believing without seeing is "blessed" (20:29). Why the difference? Because not everyone who believes can possibly have firsthand experience of the empty tomb. This was true for Thomas and would be true for all those coming after him who are reading the Gospel of John and learning about Jesus.*

*According to Luke 24:13–32, Jesus appeared first on the road to Emmaus and then to the disciples. It was here that he began clarifying the connection between Israel's story and his resurrection. Jesus explained that his resurrection was part of God's plan in the Old Testament (v. 25). It would be the apostle Paul who would do the most in clarifying the deep significance of it all. Jesus' resurrection is not a last-minute trick God pulled off to show how powerful he was. Rather, it is the heart and center of the Christian faith. The way Paul puts it is that Jesus is the "firstfruits" (1 Corinthians 15:20, 23) of the resurrection of believers. His resurrection is "phase one" of a grander plan of God to fully redeem his people from death. In other words, the resurrection of Jesus is an indication that the curse of death, the ancient enemy of the Garden, is defeated.*

*The resurrection of Jesus is like a thread that runs through the entire New Testament and draws it all together. As the student grows older, we will uncover more and more of the significance of the Resurrection. At this stage, however, it is sufficient that children be introduced to the Resurrection. The focus of this passage is on the fact of the empty tomb.*

*Begin the lesson by reading aloud:*

> Early on the first day of the week, while it was still dark, Mary Magdalene went to the tomb and saw that the stone had been removed from the entrance. So she came running to Simon Peter and the other disciple, the one Jesus loved, and said, "They have taken the Lord out of the tomb, and we don't know where they have put him!"
>
> So Peter and the other disciple started for the tomb. Both were running, but the other disciple outran Peter and reached the tomb first. He bent over and looked in at the strips of linen lying there but did not go in. Then Simon Peter, who was behind him, arrived and went into the tomb. He saw the strips of linen lying there, as well as the burial cloth that had been around Jesus' head. The cloth was folded up by itself, separate from the linen.
>
> Finally the other disciple, who had reached the tomb first, also went inside. He saw and believed. (They still did not understand from Scripture that Jesus had to rise from the dead.)

Jesus was buried in a tomb after he was crucified. There was a certain way people were buried back then. Friends and relatives would wrap the body in strips of expensive linen cloth with spices to take some of the smell away. A cloth was also placed over the face of the dead person. Then the body was laid in a tomb, often a small cave carved out of a rock, and a large boulder was rolled over the front of the tomb. An important reason for using a large boulder was to keep grave robbers from coming in and taking the expensive linen or other things that the family might have left in the tomb. (Grave robbers were common in the ancient world. For example, you have probably heard of grave robbers breaking into the pyramids to rob the graves of pharaohs in ancient Egypt.)

All of this preparation took a lot of time, and this was a problem for Jesus' followers. Jesus was crucified on Friday, and he died in the afternoon. Just a couple of hours later, the sun would go down. That was when the Jewish Sabbath began. The Sabbath lasted from sundown Friday until sundown Saturday—24 hours. During that time Jews were not allowed to do any work.

That is why the disciples could not finish on Friday all the preparation to bury Jesus. They had to wait until the Sabbath was over.

Mary came back early Sunday morning, when the Sabbath was over, to finish the work of preparing Jesus' body for burial. But instead she found that the stone in front of the tomb had been rolled away—and Jesus was gone. All Mary saw were strips of linen lying on the ground. She was completely surprised, and she thought someone had robbed the tomb. So she ran back and told Peter and John. (John's name is not mentioned but he is called here "the one Jesus loved." That doesn't mean Jesus did not love the other disciples, only that Jesus had an especially close relationship with John—maybe because John was younger than the other disciples.)

John and Peter ran to the tomb (John beat Peter there because he was younger), and they also saw the linen strips lying on the ground. They went into the tomb and saw the burial cloth that had covered Jesus' face neatly folded up. That meant that no one had robbed the tomb and taken Jesus' body. A robber would not have taken the time to fold up a cloth, and he wouldn't have left the expensive linen on the ground. He would have taken it away to sell it.

The tomb was empty because Jesus was alive. He had walked out of the tomb on his own!

Jesus had told his disciples this would happen, but they did not understand. They still thought that someone had taken Jesus' body. But very soon—later that day—Jesus would show himself to the disciples. Then they would understand. Jesus was dead, but not anymore. He is alive.

# Index

Early life (Jesus) (*continued*)
family returns home, 75–77
protection from Herod, 71–75
End of life (Jesus)
alive again, 118–120
crucifixion, 107–109
enters Jerusalem, 100–102
fig tree, 102–104
outsmarts religious leaders,
104–106
"Eye for an eye," 57–60

Family (of Jesus) (*See* Brothers;
Joseph (father of Jesus); Mary
(mother of Jesus))
Fig tree, 102–104
Following Jesus, cost of, 43–46
Forgiveness, 57–60
*See also* Sermon on the Mount

Gentiles, 35–36, 94, 102
God
and Jonah, 95
as Creator, 25, 28–30, 33
as focus of the Bible, 7
as "I AM," 42
as loving and caring shepherd,
22–24
as source of Jesus' authority, 106
as the one who both saves us and
keeps us, 22
as the only one worthy to be worshiped, 90–91
"God with us" as fulfilled in the
Incarnation of Jesus, 68–70
Jesus as son of, 30, 33, 34, 35, 84,
85, 90–91, 95, 97
Jesus' miracles display the power
of, 28–30

joyful when lost sinners are found,
11–14
wants us to persist in prayer,
14–16
our humility as key to relationship
with, 19–21
our knowledge of, 43, 48, 91, 97,
106, 116
prayer to, 14–16, 41
protection of the infant Jesus,
71–73
provision for our needs, 60–64
speaking on behalf of, to someone
else, 40–41
swearing oaths in the name of,
54–57
Word of, 49–50
grace of, 19–21
Golden Rule, 63

Heaven, 17–18
Herod, 71–77
Herod (Antipas, ruler of Galilee), 31
Holy Spirit, 68, 69
Honesty, 54–57
*See also* Sermon on the Mount
Humility, 19–22

Incarnation, 68–69

James, 80
Jerusalem
in Isaiah's prophecy, 68
Magi arrive in, 72
Jesus enters on Palm Sunday,
100–102, 104
Jesus preaches in, 97–98
oaths based on, 55–57
Pilate in charge of, 117